ATEMI

ATEMI

The Thunder and Lightning of Aikido

Walther G. von Krenner

With Ken Jeremiah

www.TambuliMedia.com
Spring House, PA USA

DISCLAIMER

The author and publisher of this book DISCLAIM ANY RESPONSIBILITY over any injury as a result of the techniques taught in this book. Readers are advised to consult a physician about their physical condition before undergoing any strenuous training or dangerous physical activity. This is a martial arts book and details dangerous techniques that can cause serious physical injury and even death. Practice and training require a fit and healthy student and a qualified instructor.

First Published on March 31, 2016 by Tambuli Media
©2016 Walther G. von Krenner
ISBN-13: 978-1-943155-19-4
ISBN-10: 1-943155-19-4
Library of Congress Control Number: 2016935149

All Rights Reserved. No part of this publication may be reproduced or utilized in any form or by any means, electronic or mechanical, including photocopying, recording, or by any information storage and retrieval system, without prior written permission from the Publisher or Author.

Edited by: Victoria Tuoati
Cover Art by: Walther G. von Krenner
Interior by: Summer Bonne

ACKNOWLEDGMENTS

I would like to express thanks and gratitude to my early Aikido teachers: Ueshiba Kisshomaru (who was Waka Sensei when I was at Hombu Dojo), Ueshiba Morihei (O-Sensei), and Tohei Koichi, my friend and Chief Instructor at Hombu. In addition, I am grateful to Shimizu Kenji, who was very kind and helpful when I first arrived in Tokyo, and Takahashi Isao, my mentor and guide. Thanks also to Dr. Robert Frager, a longtime friend who provided a lot of help and support at Hombu and beyond. I am also grateful to the many other teachers I have encountered on my long Budo journey who influenced my thinking in Zen and Art, which in turn shaped and contributed to my Aikido. Their teachings live on in my Art and my life.

Thanks to Ken Jeremiah, who provided invaluable help editing, rewriting, and handling such an undertaking's frustrating aspects, and encouraging me to write this book in the first place.

Last but not least, special thanks to my wife Hana, who stood by me through all those years of Aikido and Budo training.

Walther G. von Krenner

Sandokan Aikido

PUBLISHER'S FOREWORD

In 1969, the year of my birth, the book *Aikido Complete*, by Yoshimitsu Yamada, was published. I purchased a tattered copy in a second-hand book shop after my 10th birthday, and wondered at the ability of the sensei to control his opponent by manipulating the joints of his wrist and arm. A few years later I purchased *Aikido and the Dynamic Sphere*, by Oscar Ratti and Adele Westbrook. This book has become a classic and Ratti's nimble line drawings have been borrowed and copied for decades. I befriended Oscar, and remember with love and admiration the times spent with him in his private studio in New York City.

I was able to first visit Japan in 1993 en route to the Philippines, where I was conducting research on Filipino martial arts. My first books were published by Charles E. Tuttle Co in Tokyo, so I took this opportunity to visit my publisher. My editor, Alexander DC Kask, introduced me to several *aikidoka*, including *Aikido Journal* editor, Diane Skoss, and her husband Meik Skoss, who was a student of the legendary Donn F. Draeger.

I immediately fell in love with Japanese culture, traditions and food. I made a lot of friends in Japan and relocated there two years later to serve as martial arts editor at Tuttle. I worked and lived near the Kodokan, world headquarters for Judo, and observed many classes and demonstrations of traditional Japanese Budo and Bujutsu, including aikido, at the Budokan and various Shinto shrines.

I also had occasion to visit the hombu dojo of Gozo Shioda sensei, one of Morihei Ueshiba's original students. I observed a long class for police officers and was impressed with the discipline of both teacher and student. Almost 60 minutes were spent on a single technique; a straight arm bar takedown against an overhead attack. The techniques were done with purpose, intention, and no one just "went through the moves." By the end of the session the officers' *aikidogi* (uniforms) were stained with blood around the knees, from all the hard falls. I was impressed.

Today it seems like Aikido has fallen into a "New Age" art, where going with the flow and allowing your partner to throw you is more important than mastering the dynamic movements that O'Sensei envisioned. But this is not always the case and so I feel honored to have the chance to publish a book on Aikido by Walther von Krenner, a sensei I respect and admire, who is a standard bearer of the traditional Aikido of O'sensei. With the detailed assistance of his student, Ken Jeremiah, Tambuli Media is proud to bring you, ***Atemi: The Lightning and Thunder of Aikido.***

Dr. Mark Wiley
Publisher, Tambuli Media
March 16, 2016

CONTENTS

Introduction 1

    Aikido's Striking Techniques 5

    Tohei Koichi (1920-2011) 6

    O-Sensei's Martial Arts Background 9

    The Omoto-kyo Connection 9

    Aikido's Misconceptions 11

    Aikido's Martial Efficacy 12

PART I – Shodan (Beginner) Level: An Introduction to Atemi-Waza 15

    1 – Aikido Attacks 17

        Shomenuchi 19

        Balance and Centering 21

        Yokomenuchi 22

        Tsuki 25

        Grabbing Attacks 28

        Sen (Initiative) 30

    2 – Striking in all Aikido Pinning Techniques 35

        Ikkyo (Ude Osae): Technique Number One 35

        Nikkyo (Kote Mawashi): Technique Number Two 46

        Suki (Defensive Openings) and Atemi 52

        Uke-mi 56

Sankyo (Kote Hineri): Technique Number Three 58
Katatedori 58
Ju Yoku Go o Seisu: Softness Controls Hardness 61
Full Body Control 62
Technical Variation from the Same Attack 66
From a Tsuki (Thrust) 67
Consider Principles, not Form 70
Yonkyo: The Fourth Teaching 72
Targeting Pressure Points 77
Moving beyond Form 84

3 – Striking in Aikido: Throwing Techniques 89
Kaiten-nage 89
Shiho-nage 98
Throwing in Four Directions 98
Turning Four Directions into All Directions 103
Shiho-nage and the Sword 104
Strikes and Shiho-nage 106
Effective Practice 107
Sumi-otoshi 109
Martial Variation 114

4 – Putting it all Together 119
Striking Sequence from Katatedori 120
Striking Possibilities from a Straight Punch 121
From Empty-handed Shomenuchi 122
From Shomenuchi with a Sword 123
From Yokomen Attacks 124
From a Round-house Punch 125
Possible Entries and Strikes for Kicks 126
From Grabbing Attacks 127

From Grabbing Attacks continued	128
From Grabbing continued	129
Knife or Club Attacks	130
Other Techniques	132
Striking or Ground Techniques: The Same Mentality	133

PART II – Chudan (Intermediate) Level: Irimi 137

5 – Irimi and Other Concepts from Sword Arts 139

Shisha Tachi	140
Makura no Osae	140
Isshin Itto	142

6 – Irimi-Nage 145

7 – Aikido is 75-Percent Strikes 155

Using the Eyes	157
Mind Strikes	160
Aiki and Kiai	162
The Breath of Life	163
Striking for Real	163

PART III – Jodan (Advanced) Level: Kokyu Power 169

8 – O-Sensei's Power 171

9 – Tohei Sensei's Background 179

10 – Tohei's Four Basic Principles 185

11 – O-Sensei's Solo Training Drills 189

Conclusion 197

Notes 203

Glossary 209

Bibliography 217

INTRODUCTION

I have always been interested in martial arts, and I began studying Judo in Germany more than fifty years ago, where I trained with some great teachers, including Kondo Mitsuhiru, Nagaoka Hidekaru, and Heinreich Steffin. In 1959, a victory in my division of the German national championship provided me the opportunity to travel to France, where I trained at the famous Salle Pleyel Dojo with World Judo Champion and Olympic medalist, Anton Geesink. He amazingly won more than twenty European Judo championships. I wanted to continue training with great practitioners, so when my time in France ended, I traveled to the United States and trained at Hal Sharp's dojo, where Gene LeBell worked out.

Up until this point, I had focused on Judo, and I had never even heard of Aikido, which at the time was a relatively new martial art. One day, while teaching Judo classes at Hong Kong champion David Chow's dojo, which was located at the Encino Community Center, I showed up and learned that the directors had canceled my class so the space could be used for a demonstration of a new martial art called Aikido. Many people were there and chairs were set up, and it looked like I had no say in the matter. Reluctantly, I sat down to watch. Ueshiba Kisshomaru (1921-1999), the founder's son, performed the demonstration. He wore a *hakama*, the split skirt that characterizes many traditional Japanese martial arts, and he wore glasses, which remained perfectly in place as he seemingly threw people effortlessly. I thought it was fake, and afterward, during a question and answer session, I expressed my opinion that

> "To protect and nurture love in the world, one needs to have real and effective martial skills."

such techniques would probably not work against a skilled Judo practitioner. He invited me to attack, so I did. Ueshiba Sensei applied a basic lock and sprained my wrist. Not wanting to give up, and thinking it had to be luck, I attacked with the other hand, and he injured that one too.

After that incident, I wanted to learn Aikido, so I trained with Ueshiba Sensei until he returned to Japan. Before he left, he suggested I continue practicing with Takahashi Isao, with whom I trained for many years. He later introduced me to Tohei Koichi (1920-2011), who taught me how to strengthen my inner energy, known in Japanese as *ki*, and how to apply it in techniques. One method of testing such ki power is by pushing on each other, and there are many photographs that show both Tohei Sensei and the art's founder being pushed by others yet remaining rooted to the ground and unmoved by such pushes. Obviously, training in the martial art Aikido, I became interested in the founder, Ueshiba Morihei (1883-1969), whom practitioners respectfully call O-Sensei (great teacher). He was an amazing individual who trained in various martial arts until he met Sokaku Takeda (1859-1943), the eminent Daito-ryu Aikijujutsu instructor. (More information about this martial art will be provided in forthcoming chapters.) According to O-Sensei, Takeda Sensei opened his eyes to Budo, or true martial arts. After training with him, O-Sensei devoted his time to perfecting Daito-ryu techniques; he also engaged in solo training drills to build an Aiki body. (An Aiki body refers to one that is more connected; this is necessary to apply full-body control and power.) These days, few practitioners still engage in such practices. Later in life, he became involved with the Omoto-kyo religion, and he combined his martial and spiritual pursuits into one path: one martial art that he believed could unite people worldwide. He called it Aikido.

> "O-Sensei combined his martial and spiritual pursuits into one path: one martial art that he believed could unite people worldwide."

In 1967, while I was still in the United States, Takahashi Sensei came to my house and suggested that I go to Japan while O-Sensei was still alive. I didn't have to think about it for long before deciding that I did want to train with him. My wife Hana was supportive, and we sold our home to free up some much needed traveling funds. I headed to Japan to train with the art's founder, and I stayed there for the last two years of his life. Some of the pictures in the book *Training with the Master* are from this time. I also took copious notes about O-Sensei's classes, techniques, and his hard-to-follow lectures. Most of this information, along with some great photographs of this time, will appear in the forthcoming book *Following the Spiritual Path*.

O-Sensei's Aikido was different from the type of Aikido that many students and teachers practice these days. His ideals of peace and harmony seem to have supplanted modern practitioners' desire for effective techniques and fighting skills. They view the founder's spiritual goals as more important than the art's physical techniques. However, this is a mistake. O-Sensei never disregarded martial efficacy for spiritual and religious goals. In fact, to him, the development of martial skills was not just important but downright necessary; how else could someone truly control a violent, out-of-control person? To protect and nurture love in the world, one needs to have real and effective martial skills.

Many pictures of O-Sensei show him grappling on the ground in positions that are generally not practiced in modern Aikido, and they also show him using strikes. Strikes are available and present in every technique, and when I attended his classes in Japan, his strikes were palpable, even if onlookers didn't see the actual movements. Strikes in Aikido serve many functions, and they flow with the techniques themselves, making them difficult to spot. Perhaps this is why O-Sensei occasionally went out of his way to blatantly show a strike and its intended target. He said that Aikido was 75-percent striking, indicating that it is the art's most important component. For this reason, Aikido practitioners who truly follow the founder should spend 75-percent of their practice time using strikes, learning how to strike with power, and figuring out how strikes fit into Aikido techniques. Unfortunately, such training is not undertaken at many dojo these days, and visitors might not see a single, real strike during an Aikido class.

Before people begin training in a martial art, they usually stop by to watch a class. When potential students attend an Aikido class, they generally note the following: the first fifteen or twenty minutes are spent on stretches and warm-ups. Then, students kneel in a row and the instructor picks one of them, who reaches out and grabs his teacher's wrist, as though trained to do so in a Pavlovian way. The teacher then demonstrates some kind of blending exercise, such as *tai no henka* (body-changing practice). Sometimes he speaks, explaining things in detail, but more often, the instruction is imparted silently. He expects students to watch carefully and emulate his movement. After demonstrating this four or more times, the instructor beckons the students to practice. They pair up and quietly perform the same exercise. After ten minutes or so, the teacher claps his hands and the students line up again, waiting for him to demonstrate a new exercise or technique.

Building on the initial blending exercise, the instructor might choose the same attack: a wrist grab. He might use the same body movement, but now he turns it into a technique like *kotegaeshi* (wrist-turning technique). He perhaps does it slowly, emphasizing correct body motion and *maai* (spacing). Eventually, he moves quickly, adhering to the same base principles, which the students had spent the first part of the class practicing. All the while, potential students are watching and getting the perception that Aikido does not have any strikes. How shocked they would be to learn that Ueshiba Morihei said Aikido is 75-percent striking! Other Aikido instructors, such as Saito Morihiro (1928-2002), claim that 99-percent of Aikido is striking.

It is perhaps at this point that the instructor turns the initial wrist grab into a straight thrust. A fighter watching the class will note how the attacker strikes. In many Aikido dojo, practitioners are not taught how to strike with power. They often strike in an ineffective manner, in which they are double weighted. This means they are not centered and connected to the ground when they strike. Therefore, it is easy to unbalance and then throw or pin them. A fighter, or even another martial artist who spars, will wonder how effective Aikido's defensive techniques are against real strikes, considering that its students do not seem to practice them. These observers, perhaps gaining a false impression, might be shocked to read about early Aikido students, who defeated challengers with Aikido's powerful strikes: strikes that seem non-existent in many modern dojo.

Gozo Shioda Sensei (1915-1994)
Photo courtesy of Site Officiel Fédération Aïkido Yoshinkaï de France and the International Yoshinkaï Aïkido Federation, made available as part of the Wikimedia Creative Commons. Source: https://commons.wikimedia.org/wiki/File:Gozo_shioda.gif

Aikido's Striking Techniques

Shioda Gozo (1915-1994) wrote about a fight in Shanghai. He was up against several large Chinese men. Shioda fought alongside a man named Uraoka, a fourth-degree Judo black belt. According to Shioda, Uraoka fought beautifully, using techniques like *hanegoshi* and *uchimata*, but every time he threw someone, the Chinese attackers just got right back up. Shioda commented that this was because Uraoka lacked decisive finishing techniques, which Aikido practitioners have in their repertoire. Shioda wrote:

> "I decided I wanted to test just how effective an Aikido striking technique could be, so I said, "Let me give him a try!" When the guy, who had just been thrown again by Uraoka, got up and came at me, I drove a single shot into his ribs. He groaned as he bent backwards and then he collapsed, frothing at the mouth."[1]

When dealing with other attackers, Shioda's powerful strikes caused serious damage. He explained:

> "There were still three of them left. One of them, a big Chinese guy, suddenly came and drove a kick at me. I opened my body to the left and struck his leg with my right hand as I turned my back to him. My movement just happened naturally. I didn't think about it all and I certainly didn't put a lot of power into it. And yet, the guy dropped right to the floor. I found out later that his knee joint and bones were broken."[2]

Shioda was not unique in this regard. Many of the founder's students were known as not just skilled martial artists, but also possessors of internal strength and powerful striking techniques. Such students include Shirata Rinjiro (1912-1993), Tomiki Kenji (1900-1979), and Tohei Koichi.

Tohei Koichi (1920-2011)

Tohei was one of the most influential Aikido teachers in the world, and he did more to establish the art internationally than anyone else. He even named the modern techniques. *Ikkyo*, *nikkyo*, and *sankyo* were called *ude-osae*, *kote-mawashi*, and *kote-hineri* while O-Sensei was alive. Tohei Sensei switched the terminology to make the art more accessible for non-Japanese students. He was the chief instructor at Hombu Dojo in Tokyo for many years, and his contributions should be recognized and praised. He was, without doubt, the most important figure in Aikido's post-war history. Stan Pranin described him during this period:

> "Indulge me for a short while as we board together a time machine to the golden years of Aikido's infancy in the U.S.A. in the mid-1960s. We see a different landscape when

Tohei Koichi (1920-2011) Credit: ©Walther von Krenner

compared to the art of today. The name of Koichi Tohei is on everyone's lips. He is now in his vigorous 40s, handsome, charming, and physically gifted. He is a fluent speaker of English, the author of best-selling books on the art. He is supremely confident, a wonderful teacher. He is the chief instructor of the world headquarters' dojo, the Mecca of Aikido, and he is the "ambassador of ki." Yes, Koichi Tohei is the man every devotee wants to see in the flesh, the one whose techniques are to be emulated, the one who inspires. His interpretation of techniques represents "the" standard. His views on the principles of Aikido and the "mysterious" concept of ki are unending topics of conversation. He is the motive power driving the spread of the art. Koichi Tohei *is* Aikido!"[3]

Tohei concentrated his martial studies on internal energy, and he was so powerful that others were unable to throw him. He, like O-Sensei (Ueshiba Morihei), was known for his explosive power, which manifested in throws and strikes. While introducing the art to people in Hawaii, he faced strong practitioners of Judo and other martial arts who wanted him to prove Aikido's efficacy. Once, he even fought seven people at once, and he came out on top. He developed his power through the study of Aikido, in which O-Sensei taught him how to relax, and through other solo training in which he developed internal power and Aiki. Tohei explained:

> "When you are truly relaxed, your entire body can become quite solid when you want it to be. People who try to build up their muscles can only generate power in certain places and in certain ways. Being relaxed allows people to use their strength in a much more comprehensive manner. When someone tries to run into me, I can make my whole body become like iron for an instant and send him reeling back. For that reason, karate punches and the like don't really have much effect on me."[4]

Many of O-Sensei's (early) students had the ability to channel extreme power into their strikes, and to remain rooted to the ground with an energy-infused body, making it nearly impossible for others to throw or easily damage them with strikes.

By looking at the art's history, certain questions surface that some choose to disregard. True Aikido students must wonder what happened to such power, since modern Aikido practitioners do not seem to have such abilities, nor do they know how to develop it. Even the general idea of *atemi* (striking) in Aikido seems to have changed. While O-Sensei said that Aikido was 75-percent strikes, many modern instructors do not teach people how to strike with power. Some beginning students even think that Aikido does not have any strikes. What happened? Many modern students and instructors of the art would initially chalk this up to changes that have occurred throughout time, changes that the founder himself might have initiated. It is certainly true that Ueshiba changed the martial arts that he studied to formulate Aikido.

O-Sensei's Martial Arts Background

O-Sensei had always been interested in the martial arts, and he associated with many high-ranking military officers. He was even in the military himself, serving in Manchuria during the Russo-Japanese War as a member of the 61st Army Infantry Regiment of Wakayama. It is said Ueshiba killed bandits with his sword. However, this was not the beginning of his fighting career. While young, O-Sensei trained in Tenjin Shinyo-ryu Jujutsu and Yagyu-ryu Jujutsu, but it was his run-in with Takeda Sokaku that opened his eyes to the martial arts' true power and significance. O-Sensei learned two important concepts from Takeda, and they were independent of physical techniques. These were the principles of Aiki and internal power, both of which result in incredible martial prowess. As Ellis Amdur pointed out, "What Ueshiba referred to and demonstrated as Daito-ryu Aikijutsu was the instantaneous exertion of untraceable, unstoppable force."[5] After a short period of study, O-Sensei began teaching Daito-ryu. He was known for his powerful strikes. Explosive power was also released in his techniques and solo training exercises, evidence that he developed techniques of power generation while training with his teacher. Eventually, he merged the powerful martial techniques that he learned with spiritual practices. It was not until he began studying the Omoto-kyo religion that Aikido, as it is known today, was born.

The Omoto-kyo Connection

Omoto-kyo is a Shinto-based Japanese religion grounded on the teachings of Deguchi Nao (1836-1918), an illiterate woman who was allegedly possessed by a deity called Ushitora no Konjin. She picked up a brush and wrote the absurdly long holy text called *ofudesaki*. (It is approximately 200,000 pages in length!) She was unable to read what she had written herself, but the text became the faith's base. Deguchi Onisaburo (1871-1941), her son-in-law, became the religion's head, and it was largely due to his actions that Omoto-kyo became so widely known. He was an unusual character, often claiming that he was the incarnation of various Buddhist and Shinto deities. He professed that he was the Mongolian Khan, Sakyamuni, the Dalai Lama, and even Maitreya, the future Buddha.

Deguchi Onisaburo (1871-1948)
Credit: Image is in the public domain, made available as part of the Wikimedia Creative Commons. Source: https://commons.wikimedia.org/wiki/File:Onisaburo_Deguchi_2)

Ueshiba became Deguchi's friend and confidant, and served as his personal bodyguard. While defending Deguchi during an unsuccessful journey into Mongolia, where they planned to take control of some property and establish a new "heavenly kingdom on Earth," Ueshiba killed bandits with his sword. He also continued to perfect his martial abilities while living at the Omoto-kyo compound in Ayabe. He practiced solo exercises designed to increase his internal power, and eventually, he formulated his own martial art, which embodied Omoto-kyo principles. He combined these with the internal techniques that Takeda taught him. The name of the art, Aikido, was suggested by his spiritual teacher Deguchi. If it were not for him, Aikido as it is known today would not exist.

O-Sensei did not leave the faith until years later, when the Japanese government, which regarded Omoto-kyo as a divisive cult and national threat, initiated what is now known as the Omoto Incidents. The first occurred in 1921, the second in 1935, which led to its temples' burning and its clergy's incarceration. Even though he left the faith, Ueshiba still clung to its spiritual teachings. It is likely that he perceived a connection between Aiki, internal power, and spiritual practices. In other words, he understood that there was a correlation between individual energy and universal energy. This perhaps led him to declare, "I am the universe."

Aikido's Misconceptions

What O-Sensei did, combining the martial and spiritual paths, was not unique. Many martial artists have done the same, including Kano Jigoro (1860-1938), Judo's founder and one of O-Sensei's idols. He said, "I believe that world peace and the welfare of humankind must be realized through the spirit that Judo brings about." However, something that might be unique about Aikido is the prevalence of various misconceptions regarding its martial efficacy. Some who train in the art believe that Aikido is not a martial art. Such people are unaware of O-Sensei's teachings and the true nature of its techniques. Others think that Aikido is a martial art, but since it is an art of peace, it contains no strikes. This too reveals an ignorance of the art's underlying principles.

The most common misconception regarding Aikido's martial efficacy is that there was a huge difference in techniques between pre-war and post-war Aikido. Certainly, some of the techniques look different, as they changed naturally as time progressed, but the underlying principles remained the same. They are grounded in the high-level teachings conveyed in Daito-ryu Aikijujutsu, and they were supposed to be passed down through Aikido. However, after O-Sensei died, his son Ueshiba Kisshomaru opened Aikido to the world. It took on another function. As the founder himself said, "Aikido's role is to link the world together through harmony and love."[7]

Many practitioners who view the changes that took place throughout the decades believe that O-Sensei's comment regarding strikes in Aikido (that they are 75-percent of the art) was made early. They think that strikes were an important part of the art before the war, yet after they were not. However, history does not support this assumption. The founder continued to stress the importance of striking until his death. And while it is undeniable that Aikido has changed a great deal, any modern practitioners who devalue striking techniques are not training in the art that Ueshiba Morihei taught. The use of atemi in Aikido techniques has simply been misunderstood. An online search using phrases like "striking in Aikido" reveals just how pervasive this misunderstanding has become, as few examples exist.

Aikido's Martial Efficacy

Some writers pose questions on blogs, asking about the art's martial efficacy. They claim things like, "Aikido does not have any real strikes or ground fighting techniques, so it is likely that practitioners cannot adequately defend themselves against other martial artists."[8] Others counter such claims, writing things like, "Aikido can be used in real fights, and it has limitless applications. However, such applications are not explicitly taught. They slowly emerge as one studies the art for years." Examining the techniques and teachings of some high-ranking practitioners shows that this latter defense is not always accurate. It seems that if concepts are not explicitly taught, they are not understood. Before World War II, the Aikido dojo in Tokyo was called Hell Dojo because of the intense practice that took place there. Striking within techniques, and strikes functioning as techniques in and of themselves were taught. They were commonplace, and as such, Aikido students were known as powerful martial artists. Aikido was known as one of the most effective martial arts in Japan. Today, this view has faded, and questions abound regarding Aikido's martial efficiency. Teachers do not even concur regarding the nature of atemi. While some high-ranking teachers claim that striking is the heart of the art, others claim Aikido has no strikes. Still, others view striking as destructive, and they believe it runs counter to the religious ideals that O-Sensei tried to instill in the art during its formative years even though Ueshiba stated repeatedly that Aikido is Budo. Such incongruity only exists because modern-day practitioners do not understand the art of striking and how it fits into the performance of basic and advanced techniques. Curious students might become even more confused if they sought answers to such questions, since there are no other books about the subject in English.

This book, *Atemi: The Thunder and Lightning of Aikido*, reveals atemi's true importance in Aikido techniques, and also how to teach it. Like everything else, it should be taught in a systematic manner, and there are different levels of understanding. This book is organized so that readers begin learning basic striking applications in Aikido techniques (shodan level). This level encompasses the ability to use strikes throughout pins and throws, which can unbalance the opponent or make space, giving the practitioner time to apply controlling techniques. It also involves the true meaning of both *ate-mi* and *uke-mi*, and their relationship to striking.

Then, progressing from this beginning stage, readers will come to understand that atemi is the very heart of Aikido. Striking is within each technique. It *is* each technique, and although sometimes the *ate* (strike) is visible, many times it remains unseen. However, its presence opens the door to a myriad of techniques. This notion of atemi is intricately related to the concept of *irimi* as it was taught by Aikido's founder. This is an intermediate understanding (chudan level), which in turn can lead to advanced levels (jodan). The higher levels make use of appropriate timing, and the development of a connected body, which can be used to issue powerful blows. O-Sensei had such skills, and he passed these competences to his students, even though they are rare among modern practitioners. Those studying Aikido must strive to develop such expertise and incorporate O-Sensei's training methods into their own daily routines. This is the only way in which Aikido can be passed down to future generations. If modern instructors allow this portion of the art to slip away, it will eventually be forever gone, and Aikido will become a useless dance, while its practitioners delude themselves and think that they are training in a martial art or Budo.

"If modern instructors allow this portion of the art to slip away, it will eventually be forever gone, and Aikido will become a useless dance."

This is the most comprehensive book in existence on striking techniques in Aikido, and it is hoped that readers take the lessons presented within and incorporate them into their training. In this way, we will all truly follow

O-Sensei, and we will preserve his art, so that it can continue into the future. Some may think that they are familiar with the striking basics, and want to skip directly to the intermediate or advanced sections of this text. However, it is suggested that readers avoid this temptation. While it is certainly true that some basic concepts introduced in this first chapter will be readily understood, it is important to comprehend how these concepts are explained and perceived by the writers, so there are no misunderstandings further in the text.

PART I
SHODAN (BEGINNER) LEVEL:
AN INTRODUCTION TO ATEMI-WAZA

Hogejaku: Throw it All Away. One must remove preconceived conceptions to see things clearly.
Credit: Calligraphy by Walther G. von Krenner

1

AIKIDO ATTACKS

To an outside observer (not just outside Aikido, but all martial arts), the idea of striking likely seems straightforward: that it is nothing more than hitting an object. Beginning martial arts students perceive more. They realize that unlimited methods of delivering strikes exist, and there are different reasons for striking. For example, a strike to a vital area might be used to inflict severe injury or death, while a strike to another area might be a ruse, getting the opponent to react in a certain way. Or, a strike could be an unbalancing movement. Already, the concept of strikes is beginning to sound more involved and difficult, but this is still a base-level, beginner's understanding of how strikes can and should be applied in martial situations. Sometimes, after studying a martial art for a decade or less, practitioners begin to think they have some skill, and they do not delve deeper. They do not probe the deepest recesses of the art that they are studying, and they stagnate. They may get higher ranks and even begin teaching the art, but their understanding of all aspects, including the specific aspect of atemi, is lax. If practitioners never think they are good, if they always consider themselves beginners, a greater understanding will develop.

As martial artists' skill level increases, they begin to consider the direction of force and realize that its unidirectional application is unwise. It is far better in punches and kicks to have multi-directional forces, which creates *fure-Aiki*, an important concept in Daito-ryu Aikijujutsu and Aikido. Obviously, the more students study such concepts, the more they realize there is no end to the pursuit. This initiates the change between the lower levels of the martial arts and the higher, secretive levels, which were traditionally revealed to only a select few. Any aspect of the martial arts, when thoroughly understood, could make up an entire volume of texts, and it is therefore easy to want to dive into the middle of them, without the requisite, basic knowledge. This is especially true for those who have been training in Aikido or other arts for several years or more.

In many dojo, strikes are taught differently, if they are taught at all. In addition, Japanese terms are used diversely. Japanese speakers use them as the terms are properly defined in the Japanese language. Practitioners who do not understand the Japanese language, but who choose to use it anyway in their respective dojo, often end up confused about the true meaning of some terms. Without engaging in high-level studies of their arts, the terms seem easy to understand. Students who never gain the deeper meaning or significance of these terms end up having a one-dimensional understanding of them. Therefore, although advanced students will certainly review some basic terms and concepts that they already know well, it is suggested that they do not skip the first sections of this text.

Before exploring atemi's complex uses, it is necessary to explain the basics. Typically, in Aikido dojo, like in other traditional martial arts, the person who is attacked (the one who will eventually do the technique) is called either *nage* (thrower) or *tori* (doer or taker). The person who attacks is called *uke* (receiver). This is because he will eventually be thrown, pinned, or counterattacked, thus receiving nage's action. In many Aikido dojo, uke is classified as the attacker, while nage defends. Obviously, in any realistic combat situation, such divisions do not exist. The attacker does not just attack, nor does the defender simply protect himself. Each participant uses both attacks and defenses. The two become one, and both defender and attacker cease to exist. Whoever has the greatest martial prowess will come out on top. However, it is reckless to just throw beginners into such a bout, expecting them to gain this level of understanding. For this reason, the distinctive roles of attack and defense are delineated.

There is another reason for this separation in Aikido and some other martial arts. The arts are not all about fighting, and some great fighters who have never studied a so-called martial art can trounce some high-ranking martial arts instructors. The techniques are designed to convey principles, which are more easily understood when there is a clear division between attack and defense. These principles, depending on the art, might be physical or spiritual, but it is certain that they are deep concepts, not understood by anyone without decades of training. In some traditional martial arts, the highest, secretive principles were embedded into the very first technique. After years of training, the underlying aspects become clear. O-Sensei said that Aikido had no techniques. When he moved, techniques were born. The techniques one sees in Aikido are just possible conclusions to the initial body movements and underlying principles. They are manifestations of the principles, and should be interpreted as such. Keeping this in mind, it is possible to demonstrate ikkyo, nikkyo, sankyo, and all other Aikido techniques through strikes alone. In other words, while being attacked, the nage can use the principles of ikkyo (and other techniques) to counterstrike. Clarifying the roles of attacker and defender in the dojo helps to highlight each technique's base principles, so they can be passed on to serious students. The defender adopts a stance, and uke attacks. Traditional attacks in Aikido are based upon sword movements. Striking attacks include *shomenuchi*, *yokomenuchi*, and *tsuki*.

> "If practitioners never think they are good, if they always consider themselves beginners, a greater understanding will develop."

Shomenuchi

Shomenuchi is a vertical attack issued with the hand blade (*shuto* or *tegatana*). With an actual sword in one's hand, the attack would be delivered by holding the sword directly over one's head and then cutting straight down, maintaining the body's center and aiming at the opponent's forehead. Anyone familiar with Japanese history and the use of swords on Japanese battlefields will realize that this attack does not make much sense. Samurai wore armor. Their large helmets and shoulder guards prevented them from lifting swords directly over their heads. Shomenuchi attacks were therefore issued from *in no kamae*, also known as *hasso* posture, or from a position in which the hands were in front of rather than directly over the head: a position called *jodan*. In addition, intentionally striking the opponent's protected head is illogical. Old sword arts, tested on ancient battlefields, always exploited the armor's weak points.[9]

Uke (Lucas Brown) strikes with shomenuchi, while nage counters with a strike to the ribs.

It is useful to keep this in mind when trying to understand the true purpose of Aikido attacks. They are not real attacks, but only movements that are strong in specific directions. By dealing with such power and learning to redirect it, students can eventually defend themselves using the same techniques against real attacks, which are issued more quickly against more vulnerable targets. When uke strikes with shomenuchi, he generally steps forward and strikes with the forward hand. In some dojo, attackers do not step forward at all. Instead, they slide the front foot forward so that they can reach their target, and then they strike with the front hand. No matter what footwork is used initially, when a shomenuchi strike is launched, the ending position is one in which the hand and foot on the same side of the body are forward. If the right hand is striking, the right foot is forward.

Balance and Centering

This position is logical when considering swordsmanship, as such a posture generally creates more reach (more distance that can be covered with the blade). But beginning students typically strike in a way that makes them unstable, and they are easily unbalanced while striking. It is important to guard against this, and to always maintain one's center. Performed incorrectly, at the conclusion of the strike, the student's weight will be on his front foot. This should be avoided at all costs. It is important to remain centered in all techniques. Whether one is attacking or defending in the martial arts, it is necessary to remain rooted to the ground rather than being light on one's feet. To accomplish this, strive to always maintain your center. When striking with shomenuchi, the tendency is to let the back knee sway forward. This is an unnatural position, and the knee can easily break if pressure were applied to the outside of it. Considering that attackers could come from any direction, make sure that no matter how you move, the knee is always properly aligned with the foot.

O-Sensei said, "Even when called out by a single foe, remain on guard, for you are always surrounded by a host of enemies."[10] Certainly, this statement can be interpreted martially. When a fight breaks out and you are dealing with one attacker, he might have friends who will attack you from behind. If you are not paying attention (if you are unaware that attackers may be approaching from behind), you will be defeated. But consideration of multi-directional possible attacks also changes your body posture. If you assume there is only one attacker, then it is only important to be powerful in one direction: the direction in which the opponent could potentially attack or recover.

> "The basics of stability and correct body movements are the key to performing more advanced techniques."

Thus, many Aikido practitioners give in to the poor habit of being strong toward their attacker, but weak in other directions.

They give up their centers, and maintaining one's center can eventually lead to more profound martial abilities. Aikido is supposed to be a high-level martial art. This basic premise, staying centered, must not be disregarded. The basics of stability and correct body movements are the key to performing more advanced techniques. Considering the position of the back knee will help many students overcome this obstacle. In Chinese arts, practitioners are often cautioned that when striking forward, the back knee's energy does not also move forward. Instead, it moves diagonally in relation to the forward attack. The knee bends over the foot's instep. Try this slowly and you will find that it forces you to remain centered. If you have been striking incorrectly for numerous years while training, you will find that you have to readjust for proper maai. This can be practiced anywhere, even in one's home, by striking something with shomenuchi and then verifying that one's weight does not shift in the execution of the strike. Make sure that you are always centered.

Yokomenuchi

Yokomenuchi connects to shomenuchi. If you are unable to strike correctly with the latter, you will also fail using yokomenuchi. Therefore, beginners should spend time practicing and perfecting shomenuchi before moving on. Yokomenuchi is a strike to the side of the opponent's head. In swordsmanship, this relates to *kesagiri*, or a kesa cut. Kesa refers to a surplice: a robe worn by a Buddhist priest. Similar to martial arts training uniforms, the left side is placed over the right side, and then it is either tied in place or secured with a belt. When it is worn, the robe's edges can be trailed at a downward angle. This line is followed when making a kesa sword cut. In Aikido and other arts that use a yokomen strike, the same angle is maintained. Generally, this strike targets the opponent's carotid artery. In this way, it becomes more martially viable when performed with empty hands.

In Aikido, the yokomen movement starts large for the sake of beginners. It introduces a new direction of power that defenders must learn to deal with, and, as they become more comfortable handling it, the strike can become increasingly smaller and more compact, hence faster. Outside the safe dojo walls, this strike relates to a boxer's roundhouse punch. The energy

Monk in Nara, Japan wearing a traditional kesa [robe]
Credit: © Ken Jeremiah

and direction of this realistic punch and the unrealistic yokomen attack are similar. By learning to blend with and redirect the yokomenuchi energy, one can (eventually) similarly handle a committed roundhouse punch. This is a common phenomenon in all traditional martial arts. To make small, fast movements, students must first train to make them big. By highlighting the correct movements, excess motions are eliminated, and speed and power naturally increase.

Typically, a yokomen attack is issued the same way as shomenuchi. Uke steps forward, raising his hand above his head, and begins to strike in the same manner as shomenuchi. As the hand moves away from his centerline and the top of his head, however, he turns his center and allows his hips to move, which facilitates the motion. This results in an oblique cut. Like everything, it takes practice to perform correctly. Many students, even those who have been training for several years, set the attack's direction with their hand and arm. In other words, the body does not establish the attack's path. When this is done, the body core works independently of the arm and hand. No connection exists, and when students later try to issue power through the ground and into their arms and hands, all stemming from the body's center, they will fail. It is important to use the body together, so that everything is connected. This connection begins by controlling hand and arm movements with the center, the *hara*. Yokomenuchi is excellent practice for this. Make sure to set the direction with the body center, and allow the hips to adjust, thus facilitating movement. The attacking hand and arm just follow along.

> "By highlighting correct movements, excess motions are eliminated, and speed and power naturally increase."

Potential problems when striking with yokomen are the same when striking with shomen. Beginners' tendency is to shift their weight and allow the knees to move into a weak position, one in which defenders can easily break their balance and perform a throw or pin. Even though the hips have shifted and the blow is delivered from a different angle, balance must be maintained. The body's weight must remain centered. Another important consideration in the issuance of yokomen and all other strikes is the head position. When the upper torso turns, beginning students turn the head and allow the hips to turn outward (as a secondary effect to the upper body's rotation). Both mistakes should be avoided.

The head remains fixed on the enemy as the body turns. The hips remain forward as the shoulders turn against it. This will result in more power. Issuing the strike in this manner also makes the defense more realistic. When the defender confronts a strong attacker whose weight is centered and low, he truly has to unbalance him before applying any technique. The attacker does not unbalance himself, just as a real attacker will do anything possible to remain strong and undefeatable while throwing kicks and punches. Defenders who train with such skillful attackers will thereby become more skillful themselves. Eventually, the Aikido techniques they are practicing will work against anyone, even resisting opponents. Such considerations should carry over into all the different attacks used in Aikido, including straight thrusts and grabs.

Tsuki

Tsuki is the Japanese word for a straight thrust. It can also be an accurate translation for the English words *stab*, *lunge*, *pass*, *touch*, and *jab*. Although there is another Japanese verb that means *to push* (*osu*), it can also be correctly translated as *push* in some circumstances. At a beginner's level, a thrust in Aikido is delivered the same way in which shomenuchi and yokomenuchi are delivered. Uke steps forward after chambering the back arm. This is the attacking arm. Then, he steps forward, planting the foot, and issues the strike. It is in a straight line, which makes it easy for the defender to deal with it. It is not a martial strike. It is rather a controlled, exaggerated movement, so the defender has a chance to practice his techniques without worrying about real injury. This method of delivering a punch yields little power, so beginning students who try to defend themselves against such attacks are not afraid. In time, they become comfortable dealing with such punches, at which time attackers begin to use more realistic ones that do not issue in a straight line.

The incorrect movements to avoid (the basic principles that must never be forgotten) involve those previously mentioned in our discussion of shomenuchi and yokomenuchi:

- ✓ Make sure to remain centered and control your leg positions.
- ✓ In addition, verify that when your upper torso turns, your hips maintain their position. Do not let them rotate, as you will be unable to generate real power, and their turning will unbalance you, making it easy for others to overcome and defeat you.

Uke attacks with (mune) tsuki, and nage counters with a strike

There are other important considerations regarding correct bodily posture, which can be more easily perfected when practicing strikes. These include the position of the shoulders and elbows when punching:

The shoulders should never rise when striking. Unfortunately, it is a problem that many people have, as their minds are trapped in their upper bodies, which means their upper bodies are unconnected to their lower bodies. The lower body is stronger than the upper, which is why we want to use it for martial attacks and defenses. One way to keep the connection between the upper and the lower body is to make sure that your shoulders remain in place, where they belong. They should never rise. Power the strike with the center, the hara, and use the lower body to support the motion. Regarding the elbows, Aikido and its parent art Daito-ryu are known for elbow power. One aspect of this profound teaching is that the elbow and the hand should never function in a straight line. Their energies are different. Obviously, when beginners start punching in Aikido and other arts, they strike in a straight line, because the attacking energy is the least of their problems. They are still learning how to stand and move in a balanced way, and how to issue power from the hara (center) while remaining attached to the ground. In time, they overcome these initially difficult concerns, allowing them to really concentrate on the elbow position while striking.

Another overarching concern while using any attack, such as shomenuchi, yokomenuchi or tsuki, is related to swordsmanship. When wielding a sword, it must move and cover ground before the wielder moves into that space. The sword moves before the person holding its body does. Although this might sound confusing, think of this from a shomenuchi perspective and it will make perfect sense. If you are facing an opponent and you raise your sword above your head, stepping in without first beginning to cut will result in you being stabbed and killed, as you are stepping toward his sword tip. If you begin to cut first, before moving, you clear a path into which you can step. Play around with this and you will begin to understand just how important this order of movements is. While empty-handed, it is the same. When issuing shomenuchi, do not move your face or body closer to the opponent's weapons without moving your hand to strike. This is easily understood. In punches too, begin punching before you step, and make sure that the punch hits its target at the same time that the foot hits the ground, if you are stepping forward. This timing is difficult to develop, but profound. Once

> "The lower body is stronger than the upper, which is why we want to use it for martial attacks and defenses."

you have mastered it, it becomes difficult for defenders to deal with your attacks.

In fact, if you are perceiving strikes and practicing their related movements correctly, you will become extremely difficult for nage to unbalance or control. This is good news for nage, as his techniques really have to work against noncompliant opponents. When uke is not easily unbalanced, he learns how to do them correctly and take advantage of the situation. Certainly, on the street, no one is going to let someone pin or throw him. The attacker is going to remain balanced to the best of his ability. He will fight to stay strong. If nage are accustomed to dealing with such (natural) resistance in the dojo, they will become much more proficient fighters. Aikido used to be considered one of the strongest and most effective martial arts in Japan. This was because its practitioners could easily overcome resisting opponents. As uke, do not try to resist nage by using force on force. This, to put it bluntly, is stupid. But, by maintaining your center and remaining heavy and rooted to the ground when you strike, your body supports itself, making you difficult to uproot, and your strikes eventually become more powerful. Training in this way makes everyone better. Such improvement begins with strikes, the element that many Aikido dojo tend to overlook. They concentrate more on the techniques that they perform, using the striker as a dummy. All it takes is a change in perception for true improvement to occur.

Grabbing Attacks

Based upon this book's title, it may seem that grabbing is outside of its purview. However, it is important to understand the origins of the attacks used in Aikido to properly understand Aikido throws and pins and how striking relates to them. Thus far, the emphasis has been on how to strike correctly. Now, it shifts to understanding all attacks so nage can properly defend against them. Aikido is most known for its seizing attacks, and when outsiders poke fun, they might hold out their hand in a sparring match and say, "Come on…Take my wrist!" Someone watching an Aikido class will see many grabs, whether uke takes hold of nage's wrist, elbow, sleeve, or shoulder, and they will wonder what the point is. Certainly, such grips could occur in realistic situations, but it seems unlikely. This is because the true scenario is rarely demonstrated in dojo and never shown to beginners.

When many think of Aikido, they hail it as a defensive art. That word "defensive" has a false connotation in which listeners immediately think that attacks are absent. Sometimes, the best defense is a strong offense. When someone is about to attack, the defender would be wise to attack himself, issuing a powerful blow to unbalance the opponent. This strike leads to Aikido techniques. It also leads to grabs. To understand this, think of the sword. After all, Aikido comes from the sword, but not the way many think. When high-level sword practitioners demonstrate their art, they perform kata, which include cuts, slashes, and stabs. Unknowing observers walk away from such demonstrations thinking that they have just seen the art. But they have not. The secret principles that characterize each old sword art are never shown publically. What viewers see is only the outward form, not the real killing motions. In traditional sword arts (*koryu*), every motion is a killing move. Things that look defensive might be, but they are also designed to dispatch the enemy. When the techniques are performed for real, rather than in a kata, something changes. The distance might be different, or the footwork, or even the angle of the sword, or the target. These secret principles are traditionally only revealed to serious students after years of study. One concept that should be understood about swordsmanship is that the first motion, the first attack, is never the real attack. It hides the real intention of the sword wielder.

> "The first motion, the first attack, is never the real attack."

Likewise, when an Aikidoka uses a strike in a real situation, the strike is often used to force a reaction. When uke reacts to the strike, techniques are born. Consider ikkyo to clarify this. Ikkyo, technique number one, is (not surprisingly!) one of the first techniques that beginners learn in dojo. Most Aikido instructors teach it in this way: Uke attacks with shomenuchi. The defender steps in while putting one of his hands just below the elbow joint and the other on the attacker's wrist. He does not grasp immediately. He blends up and over, in a motion reminiscent of an ocean wave, to unbalance and bring the opponent to the ground. Once he is unbalanced, the defender grabs. Then, he steps in and subsequently out, as though ice-skating, to keep uke off balance and to secure him to the ground. The traditional finishing pin is a kneeling one, reflecting a time in which the Japanese knelt on tatami mats more frequently that they sat on western-style chairs. This technique, performed as described above, clearly differentiates between the attacker and the defender. In Yoshinkan Aikido, the same basic technique is performed differently.

Sen (Initiative)

The person who does the technique initiates the attack. He strikes with shomenuchi, stepping forward with his front foot. The defender reacts to the strike by blocking, and then nage takes advantage of that defensive technique and applies ikkyo, (which is called ikkajo in this Aikido style). The role of attacker and defender seem to blend, but the initial attack might have been only to defend. This seems confusing, but it has to do with the concept of initiative, and the perhaps overused martial term *sen*. Tomiki Kenji, who trained with O-Sensei, explained variations of initiative, which included *sen-sen-no-sen* (superior initiative), *sen* (initiative), and finally *ato-no-sen* (initiative in defense). He wrote:

> "Superior initiative is given play in a delicate situation where one confronts an opponent who intends to attack, and gains mastery over him by subtly guessing his mentality and forestalling his action. This is the highest reach of the mental cultivation in any military art and is regarded as not easily attainable. But if you consider it more deeply, you will find it too late to try to gain command over anything when it has taken a concrete form, and you must have the mental preparedness to hold it down beforehand. For this purpose, it is necessary to learn to maintain the openness and serenity of mind as signified by the old expression, "Clear as a stainless mirror and calm as still water." Lao-tse teaches this almost divine state of mind in the following words: "It is the Way of Heaven to prevail without contention.""[11]

As Tomiki Sensei described, superior initiative is the highest ideal. Sen, or initiative, is more easily attained. It involves forestalling your opponent's attack by beginning to move first, which makes him abandon his initial attack because he now needs to deal with your motion. Ikkajo is applied after the opponent tries to block nage's strike, but nage only strikes to hinder the opponent's action, to prevent his strike. Although not easily seen, this is really what is occurring. When an Aikido practitioner strikes, the opponent might block or grab the attacking hand. This is how grabs can occur in realistic fighting situations. More advanced Aikido students train with this in mind, and they practice dealing with unlimited types of holds, both orthodox and unorthodox. For beginning students, the grabs are simplified. *Katate-dori* is when uke grips nage's wrist. If nage presents his left wrist, uke seizes it with his right hand. If the grab is cross-body, uke taking nage's right wrist with his right hand, it is called *katate-kosa-dori*. Other attacks seen in Aikido and just about all other martial arts include shoulder grabs (*kata-dori*), sleeve holds (*sode-dori*), and elbow seizures (*hiji-dori*). *Ryote-dori* refers to grabbing two hands, and *morote-dori* is when the attacker (or defender) grasps one hand (or wrist or forearm) with both of his own hands.

"You must behave as the attacker, even when you are moving in defense."

Some grabs are done martially, and their inclusion in the art can be defended from a modern fighting standpoint. Others, such as wrist grabs performed when nage is kneeling, have little relevance to modern scenarios. The attacks are typically explained as having arisen during the Edo period, when sword arts lost their battlefield function and more modern techniques, like those found in iaido, developed. If someone were wearing a sword and kneeling (or sitting informally), and he did not expect an attack (because he trusted those around him), a potential assailant might have tried to prevent him from using his blade. Therefore, the aggressor's first movement would be a wrist, elbow or sleeve grasp, intending to immobilize the defender's right arm.[13] This is the origin of some Aikido grabs. Such grips not only became a common part of Aikido, but a necessary one. Some high-level techniques, like Aiki itself (from which Aikido gets its name), are more easily learned from grips than strikes. In fact, it is hard to imagine someone actually learning how to apply Aiki without slow-motion training using grabbing attacks.

No matter which attacks are used, they are issued in a similar manner. Typically, nage assumes a posture, either standing or seated, and waits for uke to grab or strike. Then, he performs a technique. This is a lower level of training, in place specifically for beginners, which demonstrates ato-no-sen, or initiative in defense. Tomiki Sensei explained this:

> "This is not to guess the mentality of your opponent and check his action before it is done but to start an action in defense the moment you have an inkling of the offensive of your opponent. It is to avoid the opponent's attack the instant it is about to be launched upon you, and to make a counter-attack taking advantage of a pause in your opponent's movement and a disturbance in his posture. A man who takes the initiative in defense rises in opposition to the opponent's attack, and parries or averts it. Seemingly it is a defensive move. In order to stave off the opponent's attack at the last moment and restore one's position, one must keep the moral attitude of initiative so as not to get worsted by the adversary. The secrets of victory thus lie in taking the initiative."[12]

This is an important consideration: no matter which form of initiative you use as a defender, you must "keep the moral attitude of initiative." You must behave as the attacker, even when you are moving in defense. In this way, your techniques become more effective. They are not done haphazardly, and they are filled with intent. A more important reason for this mindset has nothing to do with the advanced practitioner, but for the many beginners who show up at dojo doors looking for something. Whether it is while seeking solace or hoping to eliminate fear, or searching for some kind of spirituality they have been unable to find elsewhere, people begin training to fill a void. Dojo visitors' personalities are varied, but a common reason many of them arrive is fear: fear of potential assailants, of making the right choices, of life itself. They do not want to feel victimized. It is therefore important that instructors help such people to overcome their fears. When they receive attacks, they must not do so with a feeling of receipt. They must plow *forward* and through the attacks. Train with initiative and intent. When facing shomenuchi, *enter* and control the attack. When facing yokomenuchi, do not step backward; step off the line to the inside or outside of the attack while redirecting it. Even better, step *in* and take control! Then perform a strong, decisive technique. This is psychological training in addition to the development of martial proficiency. And it is why psychological and spiritual training have always been a part of traditional Japanese martial arts (*ryuha bugei*). These two go hand in hand. Without one, the other would not exist.

2

STRIKING IN ALL AIKIDO PINNING TECHNIQUES

Learning to apply strikes in all techniques helps new students to overcome fear and to take control. For beginners and advanced students alike, strikes may become necessary for numerous reasons. If they err in a technique's execution, a strike can prevent the opponent from capitalizing on that mistake. If they do not quite have the opponent's balance, a strike can be an effective form of *kuzushi*. And, of course, if they have to deal with numerous attackers, there might not be time to apply a pin or throw. They might have to dispatch the opponent as quickly as possible to deal with the next attackers. In such scenarios, striking has various purposes. In the first two, atemi serves to make time and space (maai), which the defender can exploit to control the assailant. In the third, a devastating blow is required. It is a situation of last resort perhaps: a scenario of true necessity in which the defender must down the attacker to prevent his own injury or death. No matter what the strikes' purpose, unlimited possibilities exist for their inclusion in Aikido techniques. To explore this further, let us first look at ikkyo more closely.

Ikkyo (Ude Osae): Technique Number One

Aikido techniques are typically grouped in (what some refer to as) the five pillars, and ikkyo, (technique number one) is the first technique of the first pillar, *osae-waza* (pinning techniques). From it, these other pinning techniques emerge: nikkyo, sankyo, yonkyo, and gokyo. Due to the similarity between these techniques, and how they seem to (numerically and technically) build upon previous pins, it is likely that the founder intended to teach a sequential progression. Many modern Aikido instructors demonstrate this progression in their respective dojo. They teach ikkyo, then modify it to become nikkyo.

Ikkyo (ude osae)

Sometimes, they go directly from nikkyo to sankyo, and then to yonkyo. If the first pin, ikkyo, is properly understood, the others can also be easily grasped, as the principles that make them work are not just similar, but the same; thus it follows that understanding ikkyo's true purpose can clarify other pins' significance.

In some traditional Japanese martial arts, the highest principles are embedded into the first techniques that beginners learn, and, after years of training, they hopefully come to realize what the techniques are really about. In most arts it is rarely, if ever, the outward form. What you see is not what you get! Instead, the technique appears the way it does to obfuscate and at the same time reveal the art's highest teachings. This might seem like a conundrum. To explain further, practitioners of any given traditional art do not want outsiders to watch them train and then walk away knowing the art's secret principles. If this occurred, such practitioners might lose the advantage in an actual martial engagement. At the same time, practitioners need to continually work to perfect their techniques, while being aware of the hidden objectives that are actually at the movements' core: the real elements that make them work. In swordsmanship, it is perhaps the position of the blade and the movement of the feet that make the techniques work. The same is true for empty-handed techniques. In modern day Aikido, many practitioners, even those who have been training for decades, may think that ikkyo refers to one particular pin that looks a certain way. However, the pin's physical appearance does not make it work. Instead, the underlying principle that the technique reveals makes it effective. Since Aikido is a relatively modern invention, we have to look at the same technique in Daito-ryu Aikijujutsu, the art from which it came, to truly understand the real technique hidden by the outward form.

> "In some traditional Japanese martial arts, the highest principles are embedded into the first techniques that beginners learn."

Daito-ryu Aikijujutsu is a complex art. Its jujutsu techniques are grouped into series. Ikkajo (series number one) contains thirty techniques. Ten are seated. Five involve a seated defender and a standing attacker. Another ten are standing techniques in which the attacker and defender face each other, and five are rear attacks. Other series, such as *nikkajo, sankajo, yonkajo,* and *gokajo* are likewise similarly composed of various techniques, making up 118 basic techniques of the *hiden mokuroku*. Other technical series also exist in Daito-ryu, including 53 Aiki-no-jutsu techniques, which in turn are followed by technical collections called *hiden ogi, hiogi, kaishaku soden,* and *kaiden*. Making this even more complex is that there are multiple ways to do each techniques in the hiden mokuroku. A jujutsu version of each technique exists, but there are also Aikijujutsu and Aikijutsu versions. From each of these series of techniques, Aikido adopted only a few. Kondo Katsuyuki, current headmaster of Daito-ryu Aikikujutsu's main branch (*menkyo kaiden* and *hombucho*) explained:

> "In Daito-ryu, the first technique you learn is called *ippondori*, a difficult technique where you receive, barehanded, the frontal attack of your opponent. In the traditional martial arts, a secret technique is usually taught at the very beginning. In Daito-ryu, too, we teach a difficult technique first. This *ippondori*, I believe, has become *ikkyo* in Aikido and also is related to techniques like *shomenuchi ikkyo, katatedori ikkyo, ryotedori ikkyo,* and so on. *Ikkajo* consists of thirty techniques, but only the *ippondori* technique became *ikkyo* in Aikido. There are twenty-nine other techniques such as *gyaku udedori, kurumadaoshi, koshiguruma,* and so on. *Nikajo* also has thirty techniques and only one of them is called *nikkyo* in Aikido. And the case is the same for *sankyo*. *Yonkajo* includes fifteen techniques and one of them is called *yonkyo* in Aikido. *Gokajo* has thirteen techniques and one of them is *gokyo* in Aikido. It includes *tasudori* (techniques against group attacks), *tachidori* (techniques against a sword), *jodori* (staff techniques), *kasadori* (umbrella techniques), *emonodori* (techniques against various weapons) and so on, all of which were practiced in the old days. So we have 118 different techniques, classified as the *ikkyo* [sic.] through *gokyo*[sic.] series in Daito-ryu. These make up the *hiden mokuroku* and only five of those techniques were included in Aikido. I would like this to be clear, to avoid any misunderstanding.

The difference between Aikido and Daito-ryu in the eyes of the general public is that in techniques of Daito-ryu you must break the balance of your opponent the instant you touch him. This is because there is *Aiki* in the technique, which we use to break the balance of the opponent. This is a major characteristic of Daito-ryu. Another characteristic is its use of *atemi*. This *atemi* is also a part of *Aiki* in Daito-ryu."[15]

Ippondori, as it is usually practiced in Kondo Sensei's dojo, occurs in the following way:[16] Both the attacker and defender begin in natural stances. They bow to each other, and then the attacker assumes a fighting stance. He steps in with a shomenuchi to the opponent's head. Assuming that he strikes with a right *shuto* (hand-blade), the defender steps in deeply with his left foot, making contact with uke's arm as it rises. Then, with his right hand he strikes just below the defender's armpit: an area that would be exposed even if he wore traditional samurai armor (fig. 2.1). Then, he displaces the arm across the attacker's body, with his left hand gripping just above the elbow joint, and his right hand over the ulnar nerve on the outside of the opponent's wrist (omote side). Using the base of the index finger's proximal phalanx, (which modern Aikidoka refer to as the yonkyo spot), pressure can be applied to this point. A pressure point near the elbow can also be used if the opponent tries to resist, but the real purpose is not to cause pressure point pain. It is to control the attacker's elbow joint. As such, that is the focus of the technique's performer. He continues the movement. The shoulder is below the elbow joint. Then, he turns his hips to the left so his center is aligned with the opponent's ribs, and he kicks the opponent in this area. The strike continues, becoming a step. At this penultimate position, the opponent's arm is secured, and by keeping the arms in the correct position and moving the leg forward, slack is removed and the pin is tightly applied. At this point, the defender removes his hand from the elbow, and while maintaining the pressure point on the

> "Students must train hard in the dojo, and then return home to think... They must consider the principles behind the movements, which make them effective."

Initial atemi when performing ude-osae

back of the attacker's wrist, he strikes the back of uke's neck with his left hand-blade. Then, he steps back, releases the opponent's wrist, and returns to his original starting position in a natural stance with his palms against his thighs. Pausing a moment, uke does the same. Then, they bow to each other.

The practice of this technique, and many others, is highly formalized in Kondo Sensei's dojo. From what is known about Takeda Sokaku, this formalized routine is a new addition to the art. Perhaps put into place to teach good manners, or to assist in the standardization of techniques and bodily attitudes as the art grew and came to be practiced in diverse locations, it is not martial. The technique, as it is practiced, is also not realistic (although it is certainly painful). Instead, it appears as it does to teach certain principles. Such concepts, once understood, can be applied no matter the attack, even when dealing with a boxer's jab. First, the opponent is instantly unbalanced when the defender seizes the initiative and steps in. Then, an atemi is issued. This strike buys nage some time, and in that interval, he applies a concluding pin. A symbolic finishing strike demonstrates the technique's possible lethal conclusion, and perhaps provides a glimpse into history, when some warriors would want to cut off their attackers' heads. They needed to present them to their lords before they were paid for services rendered.

All aspects of this technique are important, including the position of the feet, the direction in which nage moves uke's elbow and arm, and the strike's timing. The finish itself is not as important, as it is just one of countless variations of conclusory pins. The strike is a constant reminder that nage could cause serious injury or death if the situation ever required it. Now that ippondori is understood, at least the omote version, consider how ikkyo is typically practiced in dojo. One minor difference between the Aikido counterpart and Daito-ryu's ippondori is that in Aikido, both nage and uke begin in *hanmi*. Uke attacks with shomenuchi, and nage slides in, taking the opponent's balance by controlling his elbow joint and wrist. It should be performed in one smooth motion, with no pause or discontinuity until the shoulder is below the elbow. In the Aikido version, uke's arm is turned, so the inside (ura) of his wrist faces up, and his elbow is forward. While in the

O-Sensei demonstrates ikkyo (ude-osae)
Credit: Image is in the public domain. Source: This photograph was taken at the Noma dojo in the 1930s, and its copyright belonged to Kodansha, which is no longer in existence. This photograph is therefore in the public domain.

Daito-ryu version the ura side of the wrist is down, and pressure can be added to the back of it. In the Aikido version, the inside of the wrist is up. The so-called "yonkyo spot" is beneath nage's hand, making it equally possible to target pressure points. Usually, this technique concludes on the ground, with nage's execution of a formalized seated pin. Keeping in mind what we now know about this pin's origin, and the underlying principles that the technique is meant to express, we can determine how defenders can use it against any attack, and why atemi cannot be disregarded. It is a necessary aspect of ikkyo and many other Aikido techniques.

> "It is amazing, in any field of study, how beginners think they understand things right away, while advanced practitioners only perceive how little they actually know."

Assume that uke attacks with a punch instead of a traditional shomen strike. This punch can be quick, in and out, like a boxer's jab, or it can be tightly curved, like a roundhouse. Consider how a good striker punches. He never overextends his arm, as such an action would expose his elbow joint to potential attacks and pins. Instead, he strikes quickly, withdrawing the arm as soon as it reaches its intended finishing position. Whether the punch landed successfully or not, a good fighter will withdraw it as intended. He will not chase after the target, thus pulling himself off balance. To deal with such an attack using ikkyo, the underlying principles must be adhered to, but the technique will certainly appear different. It might not conclude with a pin.

No matter the speed and direction of the attack, Aikido practitioners can meet it the same way. We train repeatedly to meet and redirect the attack without grabbing. If you attempt to grab a real strike, you will be defeated. Your intent should never be to grab. If an opportunity presents itself, take it, but do not go into an engagement planning to do something. Be true to yourself, and let techniques happen spontaneously. When you parry the blow, moving the attacker's arm across his body, strike. If you strike his face or neck, it will lead to omote, as his body will naturally move in that direction because of the strike. Once he is unbalanced, you may continue to pin using ikkyo. It will be possible to grab. If you strike beneath the attacking arm

Atemi to the face often leads to omote

instead, perhaps a strike to the ribs, it will cause his upper body to move in the opposite direction. This opens the door for the technique's ura version. Once it becomes available, continue the technique with intent. Do not give up. Take the initiative, and you will be successful.

In such situations, ikkyo as a pin is only possible because of atemi. When facing a boxer moving around with quick jabs, this is the only possibility you will have to apply one of Aikido's pinning techniques. Even if you are unable

Atemi to the body often leads to ura

to finish the pin, the treatment of uke's punches, in which you open a hole in his defenses and counterstrike, remains true to ikkyo's principles. The basic teachings, including body position, how the attack is met, and the redirection of force, make the movement ikkyo. This should be considered for not just other pinning techniques, but for all Aikido techniques. Each practitioner should seriously consider the martial efficacy of ikkyo's principles, and then consider the differences between ikkyo and nikkyo, which highlights a different entry and redirection angle. Then, consider the differences between sankyo and yonkyo. Remember that the techniques, in a truly martial situation, might look different, just as a koryu practitioner might not look like he is performing kata while in battle. However, the principles trained in kata are there. They are the real secrets of the art, and they are not explicitly taught to practitioners.

Students must train hard in the dojo, and then return home to think about what they have been working on. They must consider the principles behind the movements, which make them effective. For those too lazy to do this, progress will be slow. Eventually, as more advanced students forge ahead, students who do not consider such things will be left behind. They will do the same old techniques in the same repetitive way, never unlocking their true significance or potential. They will never understand anything more than the jujutsu version of Aikido techniques. Remember that Daito-ryu Aikijujutsu, the art from which Aikido sprang, has three versions of each technique, and each of those versions in turn have countless variations. The classification of three diverse versions is to highlight methodological differences, changes in approach. Beyond the jujutsu version, there is an Aikijujutsu version, and then an Aikijutsu (or Aiki no jutsu) version.

For advanced students who have begun to learn about Aiki, try these. Perform the jujutsu version of ikkyo, without Aiki. Then, the Aikijujutsu version, which makes use of the same physical motion, but the technique called Aiki is manifested throughout. Finally, use Aiki as it appeared in the previous version, but disregard the technique's conclusion, which makes it look like ikkyo. Just use Aiki to unbalance and control your attacker, while remaining true to the martial principles that ikkyo conveys. This transition highlights the change from beginning to advanced practitioners, and it takes explicit instruction and hard work. Sagawa Yukiyoshi said a stupid person could never comprehend Aiki. They will continue to misunderstand it, believing it is something like blending, when it is anything but. Strive to understand the true teachings in Aikido, both martially and spiritually, and a whole new realm of understanding will appear. The more you train and think, the more you are drawn into the wormhole, and the more concepts you will perceive as requiring study. It is amazing, in any field of study, how beginners think they understand things right away, while advanced practitioners only perceive how little they actually know. In this text, the martial aspects of each technique are highlighted, with an obvious emphasis on strikes, but keep in mind that this is just one of many dimensions.

> "When dealing with trained opponents who are striking in a rational manner, you will likely need to strike them first, before you are able to apply any kind of technique."

When dealing with trained opponents who are striking in a rational manner, you will likely need to strike them first, before you are able to apply any kind of technique. This is really entry practice, and you can train it in your dojo. Work not on finishing techniques, but on the initial blends and redirections. Certainly, "blending" is an inferior word, as what Aikido practitioners really want is *kuzushi* (unbalancing) on contact. This is not easy to attain when dealing with skilled attackers, and it takes decades to develop. But we all have decades to keep working at it! Practice entering into attacks and redirecting them. Try to unbalance your opponent upon contact, and make sure that you always remain centered. If you shift your weight, your opponent can shift you. Instead, strive to remain centered and rooted to the ground. In this way, you will become a formidable opponent.

Once you have redirected an opponent's attack, it is now possible to apply *kotegaeshi*, *shihonage*, *kaitennage*, or any number of Aikido's various techniques. When you start putting such techniques on an opponent, he will struggle. He will do anything he can to thwart your movement and thus maintain his freedom. If you are not careful, and he counters your technique, you might find yourself in a grappling situation on the ground. We dealt with this occurrence and explained how to use Aikido techniques from such unorthodox positions in our previous text, *Aikido Ground Fighting*. One way to prevent such attempts at counter techniques is to use properly placed atemi.

Nikkyo (Kote Mawashi): Technique Number Two

Looking at nikkyo in detail can help to clarify its martial application, and the inclusion of strikes in all Aikido techniques, even those done in a standard manner. In the previous chapter, it was noted that ikkyo can be

Nikkyo develops naturally from ikkyo. The same initial atemi can be used for both techniques. (uke Ryan Kashmitter)

demonstrated while exchanging blows. In other words, it can be applied in a boxing or sparring situation, although it does not conclude with a pin. When a punch comes in, use one hand to redirect the attacker's arm, making contact with it just above the elbow joint. The hand is in the same position as it is when applying the standard pin, and the arm is redirected across the opponent's chest (also like the standard version). This will affect his balance and create some time. Use this maai (spacing and timing between you and the opponent), and strike with the other hand. A strike to the face can facilitate the omote version, if it ever gets that far, while a strike to the ribs or pressure points beneath the arm can expedite the ura version. Although such conclusions are possible when facing an unskilled attacker, it is unlikely that any of these movements would decisively end an engagement with a seasoned fighter. Instead, it would create an opening (*suki*) in his defenses, into which nage could strike. Then, having struck once or twice, the fight would continue. Nikkyo can also function in a similar way.

Nikkyo, originally called kote mawashi by O-Sensei, is typically taught to beginners, but it takes years to do correctly. The Japanese term, which describes the technique, explains its gist. Kote referred to the armor that samurai wore on their forearms. Made of small metal strips joined together, kote were tied on the inside to the forearms. They protected the outside of the arms, wrists, and the back of the hands, but left the inside weak and relatively unprotected. This armor's design is why many traditional sword arts target the inside of the arms and wrists, not the outside. They aim for the opponent's weak points. (This is an important consideration overall when practicing atemi in Aikido techniques.) Mawashi is from the Japanese verb *mawasu*, which depending on the context can be translated as *turn*, *rotate*, *screw*, or *wind*. In Aikido, the technique to which it refers involves turning the attacker's wrist.

Nage begins in right hanmi. Learned from a cross-hand grasp, katate-kosa-dori, the attacker steps forward and grasps the defender's right hand with his own right hand. Nage steps out to the side with his left foot, drawing his own elbow down in the same manner as the Daito-ryu *Aiki-age* technique. He does not attempt to lift the hand and arm against the attacker's force. Instead, he moves around it while affecting the opponent's balance. This is important to remember. If nage simply moves around the attack, uke is still strong. It is imperative to upset the opponent's balance on contact. This takes years of

Kicks can be used in many places throughout ikkyo, nikkyo, and all other osae-waza techniques.

practice to perform correctly, and therefore, many Aikido practitioners like to begin moving just before contact, which makes it easier to unbalance the attacker. A Daito-ryu expression states, "Motion before contact unbalances the opponent." This is an important principle, and it must be actively researched and practiced. It should then be incorporated into all techniques. When beginners start learning nikkyo, they are not able to perform this

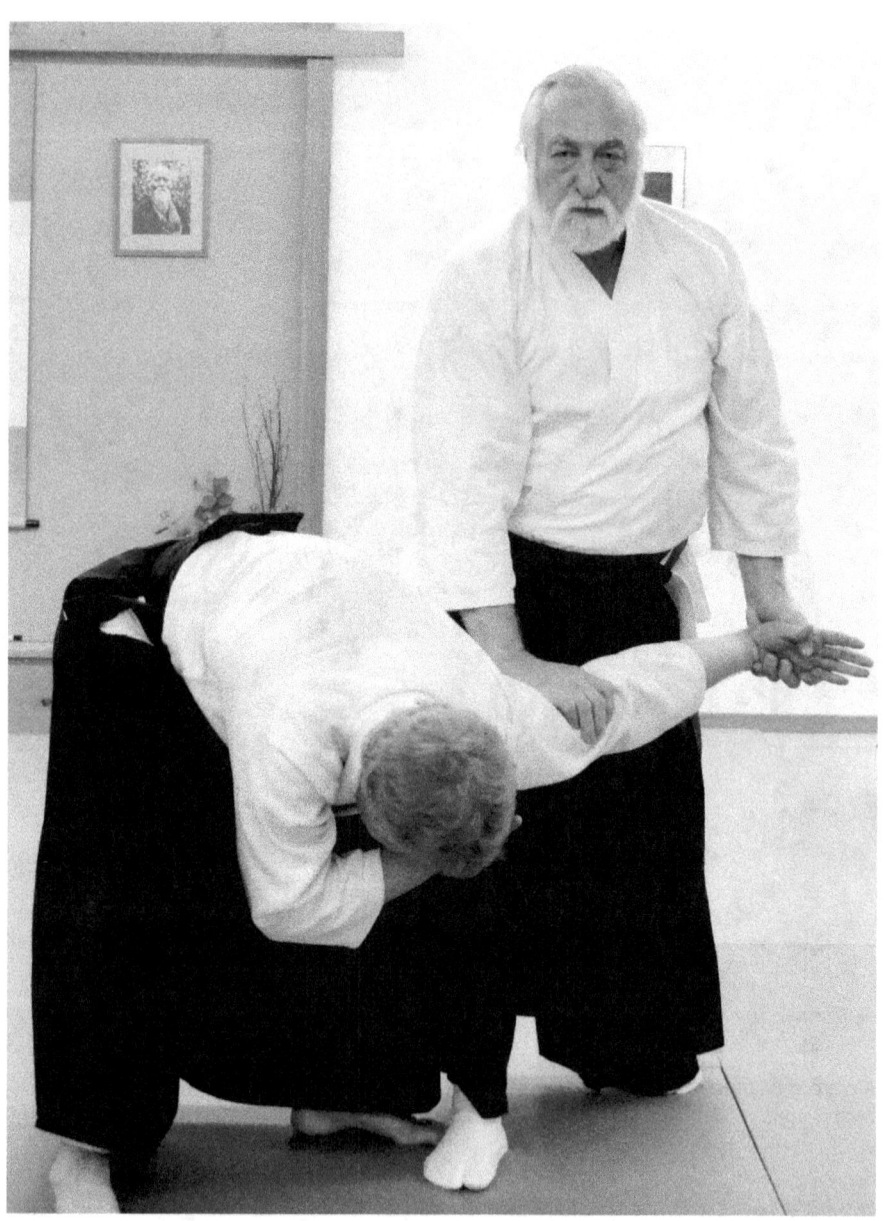

After kicking, the arm control is more easily attained.

initial motion correctly, so they will not be able to affect the opponent's balance in as subtle a manner.

However, even from the very beginning, nage moves to the side at an oblique angle. He first moves his back (left) leg, and then he repositions the right leg to protect himself from uke. He ends up in the same exact stance he started in, but now it is at an angle to the outside of the opponent's body. Nage moves his elbow down and to the inside, and points his fingers up and to the left. Then, the elbow moves to the left, which makes the fingers move to the right. At this point, the fingers travel forward and then downward, over the opponent's wrist. This motion forces uke's wrist into a weak position, and if nage continues his motion forward with downward pressure, uke will be forced to the ground. Nage should not *try* to move his partner down. Rather, he should establish the correct angle and then exploit the weakness that appears in uke, who moves to the ground on his own to escape from the technique's pain. Traditionally, nikkyo concludes with a seated pin on the ground, but numerous standing pins can also be used.

No matter which variation of nikkyo is used, there are numerous opportunities to strike with the hands, feet, knees, and elbows. (uke Rob Kits van Hayningen)

Obviously, this technique can be used without regard for attack, and strikes can be added to the technique no matter how it is used. As an example, let's stick with the same attack, katate-kosa-dori. The defender begins moving in the same direction, but this time, as the wrist-lock is applied, he draws uke toward him. The downward pressure is maintained, as before, and the correct angle between his hand and the attacker's is also sustained, but now the attacker is drawn inward toward the defender. If you are performing this technique, as you apply the lock, pull it toward yourself and slightly to the side, so that you direct the opponent's face toward your right knee. As he approaches, strike his nose with the knee. The combination of his motion and your movement, never mind the knee's strength, makes a powerful strike. You have drawn him in and dealt a brutal blow. Such a strike would likely end the engagement, unless he were able to block it or move out of the way. If he were able to pull off the target line enough, the strike might have become nothing more than a glancing blow. Considering such possibilities, do not give up the wrist lock. After the knee, you can probably apply an effective finishing pin which controls the attacker yet does not injure him anymore, or if need be, you can strike the opponent's face with your right hand. If close enough, you might sprain or break the opponent's wrist and strike his face with your fist. Applied correctly, this is much more than a damaging blow to some anatomically weak points on the face. It is the equivalent of a push, and it is used to get the opponent away. It can create some serious space, after which you can deal with another attacker, escape or do whatever needs to be done to stay safe.

> "If nage simply moves around the attack, uke is still strong. It is imperative to upset the opponent's balance on contact."

Suki (Defensive Openings) and Atemi

Considering this singular technique and the possible addition of atemi from the perspective of both uke and nage, is enlightening. First, where to include the strikes themselves is important. Their inclusion must not interrupt the technique's flow. The addition of atemi should be logical, and one must thoroughly consider where to strike and when to strike, and what happens to the opponent after he is struck. His reaction to the blow, whether it is an attempt to block it or the way his body moves upon being hit, must be understood. You cannot be caught off guard. If you decide to strike, make sure you know the potential changes that could occur (because of the strike). This can be sorted out by experimenting in the dojo, (but always remember to train safely to avoid serious injuries). Oya Minoru, professor at the International Budo University and Kendo Instructor, highlighted seven places where strikes are possible:

1. *Striking when your opponent can no longer move.* Once you deal with an opponent's attack and stymie him, you can strike to end the situation. For a specific example in Aikido, consider *morote-dori kokyu nage*: as nage, your initial movement takes the attacker off balance. You control him completely, as he now relies upon your structure to maintain his balance. Once he is in this position, you turn, and with heavy elbows, direct him to the ground.

2. *Hitting when the opponent begins to move, when his posture begins to shift.* As an example, consider ikkyo. As the opponent begins to strike, step in and control him. It is important to step in before his arm descends to perform the omote variation correctly. (In fact, it is possible that the ura version was created in Daito-ryu only to deal with the mishap of not being fast enough.) So, one does not wait for the attack, but seizes the initiative as soon as the opponent begins to move. This same movement, if the opponent stops his strike upon your entry, turns into *chokusen iriminage* (direct entry throw), in which nage issues an open palm strike to uke's chin.

3. *Attacking just before your opponent attacks.* Oya explained, "*Ki* first begins to take physical form in the movement of the sword tip and hands as the opponent contemplates and then winds up for the attack. When you discern the beginnings of movement, step in and strike."[17]

4. *Launching an attack when the opponent starts a technique.* Oya wrote, "The opponent's *ki* manifests itself in the form of slight movement. Strike at the unbalanced point just as the opponent begins technique execution (*kiriotoshi-waza*). This stage is indicated by the opponent starting to lean forward, or sinking slightly from the knees. These initial movements must be discerned immediately and taken advantage of."[18]

5. *Assaulting when the opponent has already begun his attack and is half-way through.* This is a counter-strike, or a counter-action, which halts the opponent's original intent. This pause in his motion can be exploited, and a striking, pinning or throwing technique can be applied effectively.

6. *Striking when your opponent has almost completed his technique.* Oya wrote, "Strike at the point that your opponent's psychological, physical, and technical impetus is just reaching full extension, and they are thinking that their attack was successful."[19] In Aikido, this is often the timing used when dealing with a yokomen attack. Just before the attacker's hand makes contact with the defender, he enters with an atemi and then moves at an angle, taking hold of the attacker's arm and instantly applying a technique like shiho-nage. The defender must wait, because if he moves too soon, the attacker will discern the movement and change the attack's direction and angle. Or, he will use the first attack to bait the defender, using it to hide the real attack, which is issued with the opposite hand or the feet.

7. *Hitting after the opponent has completed his attack.* This is striking when the opponent "has succeeded the point of full extension and their overall posture is ineffective."[20] Many kokyu-nage techniques are issued from this point. As uke comes in for a grab, nage moves to extend that grab, making uke stretch just a bit more. This moves him out of balance, where he can be easily thrown.

Obviously, a strike could be issued at any point in which a technique could be performed. Understanding where sword practitioners look to strike can lead to a comprehension of the same concept in Aikido and other martial arts. Aikido movements, according to O-Sensei, came from the sword. The timing of strikes issued within the performance of pinning or throwing techniques is important, and one might spend years studying and practicing before their use becomes second nature. Once a decision has been made to strike, the purpose of the strike becomes critical. Is it to injure or maim the opponent? Is it to make space, facilitating a technique's application? Or, is it to move the opponent into a position from which he cannot easily defend himself, while you maintain an advantageous position?

Keeping in mind the founder's spiritual teachings, maiming and injuring does not fit into Aikido, but the possibility must never be forgotten. Although we hope that no one will ever have to face a life or death situation, in which one defender is perhaps dealing with multiple attackers, such situations do occur. If so, a powerful strike designed to disable an opponent, thereby preventing his attack, might be necessary. Despite the defender's noble spiritual beliefs, in which he never wishes to injure another, even an attacker, such knowledge and ability to inflict damage and death are necessary. A true pacifist is one who *can* cause injury and death, but chooses not to. It is not someone only versed in peaceful techniques who could not really inflict injury if the situation required it.

So far, we have considered striking, using nikkyo as a model, from the perspective of nage, who issues the blows. Let us now consider the same from uke's perspective, as such a viewpoint will make all practitioners more well-rounded martial artists. You move in to attack the defender. It does not matter if you strike with a punch or shuto, or if you grab his clothing, arm, or wrist. He applies nikkyo, and draws you down and in, toward his knee. You know that there is a possibility of real damage, and it is likely that if you receive the blunt of such a strike, you will not get back up. The engagement will be over. Therefore, it is important to move in a way in which you are constantly protecting yourself. Never give yourself completely to your training partner. This is especially important at seminars when you train with many people who you may not know; you must always protect yourself. It is nice to completely trust others, but as martial artists, you must learn to expect the unexpected or at least be ready for it. Always keep yourself in a strong position, so if a real problem surfaced, you could take action to protect yourself. This does not mean you should fight your partner's technique. In fact, if you fought against a technique like nikkyo using force on force, you would likely cause serious damage to your joints and make your situation more dire.

> "A true pacifist is one who can cause injury and death, but chooses not to."

Rather than fight, keep your *ki* alive, extending energy in all directions. This skill will develop in time, and it will be discussed in more detail later in this text. If you are *alive*, you can move into positions in which you are protected, and you can reverse nage's techniques when a weakness appears.

The entire realm of *kaeshi-waza* in Aikido is only possible if uke does not give up. Learning to protect oneself and discovering the technical weaknesses are two reasons that Aikido practitioners blend while training. This is an aspect of *training*, not combat. After enough practice, uke will develop heightened sensitivity. He will feel his weaknesses and nage's weaknesses, and he will know how to move to remain safe. When a strong strike, like the previously mentioned knee to the face threatens, move. Rotate your shoulder and arm to alleviate the nikkyo pressure, and move laterally. Keep your other hand active so you can use it as a block as well, just in case you are not fast enough to get out of the way entirely. Even if you cannot extricate yourself completely, strive to change the angle, so that the blow's force is not concentrated on one spot. Create a glancing blow, one that does not cause grave damage. This calls to attention an important facet of Aikido training: ukemi.

Uke-mi

Uke-mi is used in all Aikido dojo, as it is used in Judo and other arts that practice throws. Ask many of these arts' practitioners what ukemi refers to, and they might state "falling." The Japanese term has nothing to do with falling, however. It means to receive (uke) with the body (mi). Considering this term linguistically provokes deliberation, as it is possible to use ukemi in other areas of the art besides falling and learning how to protect oneself when thrown to the ground or pinned. It also has to do with how one receives a strike.

"Open your eyes to the countless opportunities to strike, and they will continually appear."

In the movies, where martial art practitioners have superhuman powers, they go through countless fights without a scratch. They fly through the air and run up walls, and despite a barrage of attacks by countless enemies, they are never once struck. In the real world, things are not so easy. Even walking away from a single attacker without being hit is difficult (provided the attacker has some common sense). Though the defender might try his best to avoid strikes, some jabs or other punches will meet their mark. How one *receives* these hits is important. If the attack's full power is accepted, the defender could be severely injured or at least stunned enough for subsequent strikes to finish him off. It is therefore important to learn how to blend with attacks that find their mark, and to change the angles to create glancing blows.

Nikkyo has been explored from the perspective of both uke and nage, and the possible addition of strikes within the technique's standard version has been explained. Now that readers have this requisite knowledge, it is possible to explore nikkyo's use while punching. Ikkyo's function while punching has been previously described. Nikkyo is similar. When the attacker throws a punch, the defender parries the blow and counterpunches. Nikkyo's counterpunch is simply at a different angle than ikkyo. Many instructors teach a nikkyo version from a shomen strike that will clarify this angle. Assume that uke attacks with his right hand. As the attack comes down, nage moves off the line obliquely (and to the outside), and cuts down on the forearm with both hands. When possible, he grabs the wrist with the left hand and then strikes uke's face with his right fist. This technique is often performed while kneeling. It highlights not only the correct angle, but also that nikkyo is much more than a pinning technique.

Let's take this one step further. Assume that you are fighting someone and you both have your hands up, defending yourselves. If he strikes with his right hand, it is possible to parry his arm to the side, across his own body, with your left hand. If so, you may be able to grab his forearm or wrist with your right hand. Do not interrupt the technique's flow. Keep it going. Use your right hand to continue the motion initiated by the previous parry, and turn the arm over while dropping your own right elbow low. At the same time, strike the opponent's face with your left fist over the top of his right arm. Make your arm heavy, and think about the elbow staying low as you punch. Ride along his arm while striking, and you will find that the punch actually causes a nikkyo wrist-lock. In this way, the strike is the lock. The more you practice this and other variations in the dojo, the easier their application will be. Open your eyes to the countless opportunities to strike, and they will continually appear.

Sankyo (Kote Hineri): Technique Number Three

Sankyo literally translates to "third teaching," and it is known as the third pinning technique in Aikido. It is different from the other techniques in the osae-waza category because it forces the opponent up rather than down: a seemingly unusual concept in the martial arts, since in most arts, the primary objective of any defender is to down an opponent. However, in certain situations it makes more sense to have the opponent up on his toes. As long as you have control of his elbow, wrist or shoulder joints, his body will likely follow. Forcing him upward makes him weaker and lighter on his feet. In this way, the defender can easily lead him around, even using the attacker's body to ward off other enemies. Once he has fulfilled his purpose, the defender can cut down on uke's arm, bringing him to the ground where pins typically conclude. Before explaining this technique's specifics, it is important to understand the basic principle behind it.

Katatedori

This technique, like almost every other in Aikido, can be applied no matter what the attack, and beginners often learn it from katatedori (same-side grab); the defender offers his left hand and the attacker grabs it with his right. The defender, who began in left hanmi, moves his left foot followed by his right to assume a right stance between 45 and 90 degrees from his original starting position. At the same time, he extends energy through his fingertips, makes his elbow heavy and low, and rotates his arm as he extends it forward to take the attacker's center. Since the attacker is attached by means of the wrist grab, he "goes along for the ride." Once uke's center has been compromised, nage's right hand rises and grasps the back of the attacker's right hand. Nage controls the hand and wrist, turning the attacker's fingers toward him as his left hand slips to the elbow, temporarily taking ude osae, from which kote hineri (sankyo, or technique number three) is then applied.

Depending on the Aikido style, the transition from ude osae to kote hineri is performed differently. In the Iwama tradition, the defender contorts his own body, placing his shoulder over the attacker's shoulder to minimize this transition's weaknesses. In other styles, a wrist control learned through kote mawashi is maintained as the hand changes position. Sometimes, the defender simply grasps the opponent's fingers and drops his own elbow down,

Sankyo forces the attacker up, onto his toes.

Close-up of correct hand position

thus forcing nage upward, (which might make the most sense since this is where you will eventually want the attacker anyway).

Once he applies ude osae and maintains control, the defender uses his left hand to grab the attacker's right hand. The exact hand position appears in the opening exercises of just about every Aikido dojo on the planet: take your right hand, palm outward, and point your fingers and thumb to your left, your hand in the center of your body. Then put your left hand over the right with your fingers pointing straight in front of your body. The fingers will reach around the right-hand, grasping the muscular pad beneath the little finger. When this is done during stretching exercises, students then turn their own right hands back, thus turning their right thumbs away from themselves and the little fingers of their right hands toward themselves. This stretching exercise not only loosens the joints in preparation for Aikido pinning practice, but it also teaches students the proper hand position for kote hineri. Such understanding will naturally manifest in the technique after substantial training.

> "If you need to use your muscles to gain control of an attacker, you are performing the technique wrong, and you are thinking about the art's techniques in an incorrect manner."

The opponent's right fingers will point downward as your own left palm covers the back of his hand. Like the stretching exercise, the fingers of your left hand reach around and grasp the meaty pad beneath the opponent's little finger. Once you have this "sankyo grip," the other hand is added for further control, and the opponent is forced upward as you twist his hand and arm up and to the left in a spiraling motion. Some common errors should be pointed out so the reader can work to avoid them:

First, do not let your own shoulders rise. Your shoulders should be down, and your elbows are down. Aikido is known for elbow power, and elbow power is impossible if the shoulders and elbows rise. In addition, if the shoulders move up, they separate from the rest of the body, thus making full body power impossible. This leads naturally into the next admonition.

Do not try to control your opponent with your own arm strength. Such an action is weak and inefficient, and it will lead to a struggle, most likely with the physically stronger partner prevailing. Aikido and other legitimate martial arts never require muscular strength for success. If you need to use your muscles to gain control of an attacker, you are performing the technique wrong, and you are thinking about the art's techniques in an incorrect manner. The idea behind all true martial art systems, no matter what country they are from and when they were founded, is that the defender can use the attacker's energy to gain the advantage, control him, and then down him. Thus the weak can control the strong.

Ju Yoku Go o Seisu: Softness Controls Hardness

This principle has been explained countless times in Chinese and Japanese martial arts' texts, never mind those found in other countries' manuals. Many metaphors have been used, including a stiff tree branch breaking when snow attacks, while the young, soft and pliable branch overcomes its atmospheric adversary. Some practitioners, especially those who have been training (in any art) for decades, may grow weary of hearing such tales, but the fact that so many exist and have been preserved and passed on to modern generations attests to the principle's importance. Some Chinese and Japanese styles even incorporate the word "soft" in their names. Judo and jujutsu are two examples of this. Kano Jigoro explained the guiding principle that formed the basis of such arts:

> "Various records and accounts have been passed down over the ages with regard to the true meaning of "jujutsu," but few of them are accurate. It can be said, though, that the name apparently derived from the expression *ju yoku go o seisu*, which can be translated as "softness controls hardness." This expression needs closer attention. Let us assume I have an opponent who possesses power to the value of 10, whereas I must face this opponent with power only to the value of 7. When the opponent thrusts at me with all his energy, it follows that if I resist I will be overcome, even if I expend all my power. If, however, rather than resist my more powerful opponent, I adjust and adapt to his energy and pull back, he will fall forward under the strength of his

own attack. His power of 10 will become merely a power of 3, and he will stumble and lose his balance. I will not be pulled off balance and can pull away, maintain my stance, and retain my original power of 7. In short, resisting a more powerful opponent will result in your defeat, whilst adjusting to and evading your opponent's attack will cause him to lose his balance, his power will be reducedr, and you will defeat him. This can apply whatever the relative values of power, thus making it possible for weaker opponents to beat significantly stronger ones. This is the theory of ju yoku go o seisu."[21]

Full Body Control

Another common mistake when performing sankyo is the following: beginning students often try to manipulate the attacker's arm, and along with it, the hand and wrist. And such students who are reading this now might say to themselves, "I just read about how to control the opponent's arm by twisting it upward and to the left." While it is certainly true that this was written in a previous paragraph, the aim must be different. When you look at the technique as others are performing it, the technique looks to be an arm-control only, but this is not the case. The aim of this technique and all others found in the art is not to control a singular body part. It is to control the entire opponent, his whole body. For this reason, you must take his balance instantly (kuzushi) and when you perform this technique (and all others), do not think about manipulating one body part; instead, look at the opponent's center line. See where he is strong. Then, using the wrist, elbow, shoulder, knee, neck, or whatever other body part you control, take his balance and dominate him. When considering kote hineri specifically, if you focus on twisting his arm, you will not necessarily take his balance, and if he is a proficient martial artist, he can easily stymie or reverse the technique. This should be kept in mind no matter what technique you are performing.

Once the actual sankyo pin has been applied and you have driven the attacker upward, his weight will naturally have moved toward his toes and he will be unbalanced. At this point, you should cut down with the arm as though you were cutting with a sword, turn around using *tenkan tai sabaki*, place your right hand just above his elbow joint, and then move him to the ground. The

Once nage cuts down on uke's arm, many opportunities present themselves for finishing strikes.

formal pin is seated, but there are standing variations too. Considering what occurs when practicing this technique from katatedori, nage adopts positions that are the same as or similar to ikkyo and nikkyo before the actual sankyo pin's application. Therefore, strikes can be added at any time, as they can while performing ikkyo or nikkyo. The important thing is to make atemi count, and to do it for a reason.

If you start applying sankyo while grasping uke's right hand and then remove your left hand to strike him in the ribs or kidney, this is illogical. He is moving backward due to the pinning pain, which means your strike runs contrary to the technique's flow. This should be avoided. In addition, the

Striking opportunity in sankyo

left hand is the most controlling. Therefore, executing such an atemi does not make sense. O-Sensei always talked about blending with opponents before techniques emanate, and watching any skilled practitioner, it is easy to see their flow. Do not interrupt the flow. Keep it going. If a strike can increase or at least facilitate it, fine, use it. But if not, the technique is better performed without it.

Finishing strike

Technical Variation from the Same Attack

Other variations of this technique *require* atemi. Let's stick with the same attack for now. Instead of using ude osae and then kote mawashi before applying kote hineri, another basic variation is to apply it directly. The defender moves his body underneath the attacker's arm, turns around, makes a hand change to gain a sankyo grip, and then cuts down and proceeds with the technique as previously described. Of course, such an attack from a static position will never occur; it is a learning device. The performance of techniques in this manner is akin to kata in other martial arts styles. It is a preset form that students practice to learn proper body movements, and the correct application of pins and throws. It also helps them to develop control of themselves and others, and it allows them to explore the interplay of energies between attacker and defender. Nevertheless, if you are planning to pass under your opponent's arm, you must do something to forestall him and to make an opening so he does not strike as you move. The first movement the defender must make is to get off the attack line and issue atemi. A strike to the face followed by a strong right elbow to the attacker's rib cage as you are passing underneath will be sufficient. The first one is to temporarily blind him and prevent his strike. The second, while it could cause serious injury, is to move his body moving forward, thus facilitating the attainment of the correct hand position while initiating motion in the same direction you will take him with the pin applied.

Another possibility is to use your right leg to kick out his right leg. Kick the shin area and keep moving through. However, this kick's timing is important. It must occur as you are moving through, and it must not happen while your head and body are still in front of his shoulder. If so, the technique will be impossible to complete, and you might even injure yourself (because you are causing the opponent to literally crash into you). Space and timing, the important concept of maai, can be the key to both victory and defeat, and it has nothing to do with your partner. When training, no matter how good or bad your partner's maai is, you must do whatever is necessary to maintain proper distance. If your training partner moves too close while performing a kata, it is your job to recognize this maai breach and correct it with your steps. The bend in your front knee or arms can also fix it. This awareness in time will make you a much more formidable martial artist.

From a Tsuki (Thrust)

Kote hineri can also be applied when facing more realistic attacks like a punch. An example is in order: assume that he attacks you with a right punch. You may be able to handle the attack in a similar way to that previously described, but this is unlikely. To facilitate understanding for beginners, let us momentarily return to grabbing attacks. Although many practitioners of other arts criticize Aikido because of its use of grabs, they do not understand that such grasps are not ends, but a means to a goal. It would be extremely difficult, if not impossible, for beginners to learn techniques like kote hineri from strikes alone. Grabbing attacks provide a simpler place to start, and advanced techniques, such as the application of Aiki, cannot be easily learned in any other way.

> "Be offensive rather than defensive; you are not reacting to his attack, but dictating its shape."

Once students gain proficiency in their Aikido techniques, they can move on to more realistic attacks. For this reason, do not bypass training that uses grabs. Thinking only about kote hineri for the time being, this time make it a cross-hand (katate-kosa dori) attack, in which the opponent grabs your right wrist with his right hand.

To deal with this attack, a defender could repeat the same steps previously described, in which he unbalances the opponent, slides across the front of his body while keeping his own elbows down, and applies ikkyo. Maintaining wrist control, he switches his hands and then applies kote hineri. In many dojo, students practice in this manner; not because it is realistic but only because training in this way results in the performance of three distinct pins, throughout which students learn how to maintain control while changing techniques. Thus, it becomes a henka waza training exercise. To make it somewhat more realistic, when the opponent comes to grab you cross-handed, you can apply kote hineri directly. Move off the target line to your left or right while simultaneously pivoting your hand and arm around the contact point so your right elbow stays low while his is forced upward. Remember that unbalancing him upon contact is important, and one way to attain this is to move slightly before the opponent actually attacks. If you move in an obvious manner, he will change his attack, and the entire purpose of moving before he attacks is thereby lost. It doesn't have to be a large movement, just a small movement so the attacker has to modify his attack without realizing he is changing it. Therefore, he is actually attacking in a manner that conforms to you. In this way, you're being offensive rather than defensive; you are not reacting to his attack, but dictating its shape. This is a complicated phenomenon, and we will return to it in Section II, *Chudan (Intermediate) Level: Irimi*.

> "Once students gain proficiency in their Aikido techniques, they can move on to more realistic attacks."

In this scenario, the opponent grabs your wrist and you move across his center line, forcing his arm higher than yours and unbalancing him. Do not attempt to grab, just extend energy through your right fingertips and point them and that energy toward his center. When you do this, his grip will weaken, making available the exact spot in which you can insert your left hand to obtain the sankyo grip. Once the left hand assumes this grip, the right can be added to strengthen it. Make sure you keep your shoulders down and in place, and also keep your elbows down. Maintain a heavy feeling in your entire body, especially the elbows. Once sankyo is in place you can move the opponent where you need him. You can either cut down, forcing him to the ground, or turn and drive his elbow upward. For the most part, we want the attacker on the ground as soon as possible, so the first aim should be to cut him down quickly and decisively. If he struggles against the technique because your kuzushi was ineffective, there is no need to fight. Go with it. He wants to get back up on his feet. Fine. Blend with his motion and then enhance it by applying kote hineri that forces him up and around, and once you have gained control of his balance in this manner, you can do whatever you would like with him.

Now that this is understood, let's return to a right punch: if this is a real situation at a bar and you are facing someone who has no self-defense skills, it is possible that he will throw everything he has into that punch, thereby unbalancing himself in the process. If this is the case, it is important that your initial movements and potential strikes do not interfere with his movements. In other situations, strikes might be used to stop movement or change his direction, but if someone is coming at you hard, it is better to just use his energy to your advantage. Move off the target line to the left and toward your opponent. You actually want to enter into his attack while turning, and although a beginner might think this is a dangerous place to be, it is in fact the safest place to be. Consider that the opponent attacks with a sword. If you maintain your distance he can continue to strike repeatedly because you are still within the blade's reach, increasing your chances of being cut. When someone attacks with a sword and you are empty-handed, you want to get in as fast as possible. You want your body as close to the opponent's body as possible, thus making cutting with that blade more difficult while permitting grappling. Although not as severe as dealing with a lengthy weapon like a sword, or even a much longer weapon like a spear or halberd, punches and other strikes cannot be issued with much power from close up. If you are chest-to-chest with an attacker and he is hitting you, the power is likely coming from the arm muscles themselves. At a distance, the body rotates, which make strikes more powerful. For this reason, move in when you are attacked.

If you strike, hit the back of his shoulder with your left hand. The right arm should ride along his right arm without grabbing, thus protecting yourself from the initial attack and any possible counterattacks, such as an elbow strike or a backfist. This strike to his shoulder adds momentum to his movements and unbalances him further. From this position, it may be possible to apply kote hineri. But no matter what, never chase a technique. In other words, don't have a specific technique in mind. Such a thought will trap you and you will be defeated, especially if you're facing someone who actually knows how to defend himself. A real fighter will never put all his energy into one strike. He will never unbalance himself while striking. Instead, he will remain centered, and he will use feints like jabs to distract his adversary and force a reaction. Once he has you moving, he will issue more powerful cross punches or round houses. These strikes will be fast, and they will withdraw as quickly as they appeared, thus making grabbing their wrist or arm infeasible.

Consider Principles, not Form

When dealing with such an adversary, you must not think about applying a technique; it might be impossible. However, you can still defend yourself using Aikido principles if you understand them. They transcend techniques. In many traditional martial arts, practitioners spend years learning and perfecting kata. After years or decades or even longer, if their teachers think they are worthy, they begin learning the real art. The next few years are then spent exploring the inner concepts hidden within the forms themselves. They also strive to forget the forms. This might seem strange, so here's a simplified explanation: the forms were designed to convey principles, and students must actively practice them and study them to internalize those principles. Once this internalization occurs, they are no longer necessary. In fact, the forms hinder, so they must be cast out. Aikido has the six pillars, and the founder selected these techniques from the large corpus of Daito-ryu Aikijujutsu techniques. As previously mentioned, the pillars correspond to some of O-Sensei's spiritual beliefs gleaned from the Omoto-kyo religion. However, from a purely martial perspective, they contain principles that will make Aikido work in all situations, against any kind of attack. This understanding is the springboard that led to *Aikido Ground Fighting* and this current book.

Sankyo can be applied without a pin, just as ikkyo and nikkyo can be applied with strikes alone. Consider the energy used when intercepting an attack and then applying kote hineri. First, as the defender moves off the attack line he extends energy forward and across the attacker's center line, thereby unbalancing him for a moment. This motion requires the defender to turn his body and intercept the right attacking arm with his own left hand and arm, which is extended, while his own right hand is protecting his own center line. Then, once the defender has led the energy slightly, he grabs the opponent's fingers and applies sankyo. The defender first turns his body to the right. Once the kote hineri grip is attained, he turns to the left. Do the exact same thing, but this time forget about the pin itself. When the attacker comes in with the right punch, meet it with your left arm as you turn your body to the right. Keep your right hand and arm centered. It is active even though it does not contact the opponent's arm. Once you have exploited his energy, turn back to the left while issuing a fast, powerful strike with your right hand. This makes use of the exact same body motion as trained in various dojo through static attacks and pinning techniques. It is the same principle manifested in a different way. This is how all Aikido techniques should be considered.

This idea was explained at length in the previous book *Aikido Ground Fighting*, so we do not wish to belabor the point, but it is important to note that the Aikido trained today throughout the world is different from the Aikido that the founder himself practiced. While he was alive he was one of the most powerful martial artists in Japan. His teacher Takeda Sokaku and some of Takeda's top students were thought of as Budo gods: they had powers that other people could not understand. They were seemingly immovable at times, attached to the ground, and there are many videos and pictures of O-Sensei demonstrating this unique ability. They were also known to have powerful strikes, and they were such accomplished fighters that people came from other parts of the country to challenge them. After being defeated, most became their students. Today many think about Aikido as the "art of peace" because of the founder's spiritual goals, and while there is nothing wrong with such laudable aims, the founder throughout his entire life viewed Aikido as an art of self-defense. He never downplayed the importance of martial efficiency. In other words, O-Sensei did not supplant martial effectiveness with religious ideals. Instead, he joined the martial and spiritual paths. Both were equally important. Both *continue* to be equally important! It is up to each practitioner to make sure his or her techniques will work no matter what the situation is and no matter what the attack might be. You cannot claim to be a pacifist if you lack the means to defend yourself. Only a truly powerful person, who can issue devastating attacks and defend himself from similar strikes and kicks, can decide not to injure. This type of person alone can call himself or herself a pacifist.

> "O-Sensei did not supplant martial effectiveness with religious ideals. Instead, he joined the martial and spiritual paths."

Look beyond the set forms that you practice in the dojo. Strive to understand the principles that the founder hoped to convey to future generations through Aikido's six pillars. Those principles are formless, so learn techniques like

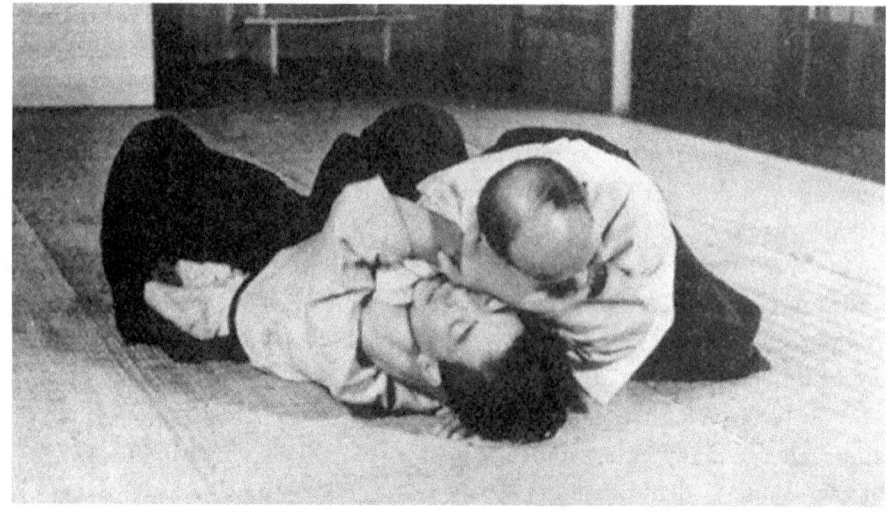

O-Sensei grappling. He viewed Aikido as a martial art his entire life. His spiritual ideals were added to his martial outlook; they did not supplant them.

Credit: Image is in the public domain. Source: This photograph was taken at the Noma dojo in the 1930s, and its copyright belonged to Kodansha, which is no longer in existence. This photograph is therefore in the public domain.

ude osae, kote mawashi, kote hineri, and many others. Get good at them. Then think about how you would perform the same techniques from unusual positions, seated in a chair perhaps, while on your back on the ground, and while fighting a Western-style boxer or a Shaolin kung-fu expert. Can you manifest the same techniques' principles in a different way so you can honestly defend yourself? This type of thinking is not easy, and it can only come about after many years of hard training, but this consideration marks the difference between an amateur and an advanced practitioner. It is the only thing you need to do to enliven your training and see Aikido and other martial arts in a new, clear light. When reading the rest of this section, which provides the background information needed to understand the points put forth in the Chudan and Jodan sections, it is suggested that readers keep this in mind.

Yonkyo: The Fourth Teaching

Yonkyo is the fourth technique that O-Sensei chose to add to his art, and it is the last pinning technique (osae-waza) that we will cover in this section. Yonkyo builds upon the previous three pinning techniques, and its connection to striking, introduced in this chapter, also builds upon previously presented information. Yonkyo can be applied in different ways. As with kote mawashi and kote hineri, beginners often learn this technique from a grab, and they apply ude osae before turning it into yonkyo. If this is done, there are numerous times when atemi can be used. You can strike at one of these points:

1. before the opponent begins to move
2. as soon as he starts moving
3. once you begin to apply the technique
4. in the middle of the technique
5. at its conclusion

Assume that you have your left arm extended, and uke steps forward to grab your wrist with his right hand. Stepping off the attacking line to the left, you can turn your own center toward your opponent's center, drop your left elbow low, and rotate your arm as you extend it toward the attacker. Take a

Proper hand position for a yonkyo pinning variation

big step forward, and, at the same time, grab the back of the opponent's right hand with your right hand and let your left hand slide to his elbow joint, taking ude osae. Your right hand can apply kote mawashi to maintain control before switching to the yonkyo grip and pin.

Consider all the places in which you can strike in this technique. When the opponent first comes in to grasp your wrist as you step off line, you can strike to his face with your right fist. As that right fist withdraws, it can strike the inside of his right elbow. Depending on how he reacted to the first atemi, this secondary strike can unbalance him even further, or it can serve to simply keep him off balance, thus easy to manipulate. As you step forward and your right hand controls the attacker's hand, you can issue a powerful strike to the opponent's ribs with your left fist. However, if you have unbalanced him sufficiently and can get your left hand to his elbow joint without a problem, it might be better to forgo the strike, since it will tend to disrupt the technique's flow. Nevertheless, it is good to remember that the strike is available. If you err and apply the technique incorrectly, the strike might be necessary to maintain control of the attacker. Once you gain control of the attacker's elbow, his ribs are once again open to an even more powerful strike. You can kick them with your left leg. This will cause serious damage, as will a kick to the side of uke's right knee as you establish control of his attacking arm.

> "Don't work on pinning techniques and throwing techniques from the first strike; instead, deal with the second or third strikes."

Once you have ude osae and the opponent nears the ground, you can switch to the yonkyo pin. If there is any resistance, turn your center toward the opponent and kick his ribs with your left foot. Continue that foot's motion forward as though it were a step and increase the distance between his hand and torso. This will remove slack and make your pin more effective. Then, you can apply yonkyo without difficulty. Of course, you could have applied this pin earlier. The opportunity for strikes only needs to be seized if something goes wrong and the technique cannot be completed without them. At the technique's conclusion, once you switch to a yonkyo grip, treat the opponent's arm as though it were a sword. With your whole body behind it, raise up and then cut down. When the opponent is on the ground, you have the opportunity to pin him without injury. If other attackers rushed in, you could maim or kill him with a kick to the back of the head. However, the philosophy underpinning Aikido prevents serious practitioners from causing unnecessary injuries. O-Sensei said that the pinnacle of Aikido practice is love, and this love must extend to fellow human beings. Put simply, do the smallest amount of damage necessary to an attacker to stay safe and gain control. Just don't forget the opportunities that are available to gain the upper hand.

If uke punches rather than grabs, the striking opportunities are the same. You can strike before he actually moves, as he begins to move, or even as his attack is nearing its target. You can step off the line of attack and issue a strike in return. Assume he comes at you with a right punch. Enter and step off the line, using your right hand and arm to parry the strike. At the same time, strike his right temple with a left roundhouse punch as your body rotates to face the same direction as the attacker. Now his momentum should be forward and you should be in a stable posture behind the opponent, your right hand and arm ready to take control of uke's arm. If this is not the case, and you are not where you want to be behind the opponent, strike again. One thing about which Aikido practitioners must be cautious is the lack of repetitive striking done in dojo techniques. In other words, they are used to striking only once before applying a technique, and they are accustomed to attackers coming forward with just one strike rather than two, three or four. This is another thing that you might want to practice in your respective dojo. Don't work on pinning techniques and throwing techniques from the first strike; instead, deal with the second or third strikes. Have uke attack with two jabs and then a cross. This type of training will pay off in the end.

You just struck the attacker in the temple with your left fist, and now you need to strike him again. Considering that you don't want to interrupt his action's flow, you have to note where he is moving. Has he continued forward, or is he now moving back in response to that forward movement? A popular Judo strategy is to pull when pushed. If you push an opponent, unless they are extremely skillful, they will push back. Once they push back, you can throw them in that direction. This is the same in Aikido. The attacker might have felt that forward momentum, and in an effort to maintain his balance, he might have moved back. If so, a strike to his ribs with your left fist or elbow or a kick to his knee with your left or right foot, might be the smartest move. On the other hand, if his balance is still slightly forward, another strike to the temple or an open-hand strike to the back of the head or neck might be all that is required to gain the control needed to apply yonkyo or any other pin.

At the conclusion of this pin, assuming that the attacker struck with his right hand, you will be grabbing his arm with both hands. Your left palm will be on his pulse, and your right hand will be just beneath the left. It is like a reversed sword grip. Swords are gripped with the right hand higher than the left. The thumbs are then rotated inward, so that the blade is controlled by the entire palm of both hands. Typically, the space between the two hands is the size of a fist. With the exception of the space between the hands, and the possibility that your hands will be reversed depending on how he strikes (i.e. which side), the yonkyo grip is the same as that applied while gripping a sword handle.

The attacker's thumb will be turned toward his own torso, while you apply pressure to the ulnar nerve with the base of the index finger's proximal phalanx. This is easy to find. Trace a line from the tip of the index finger of your left hand toward your palm's center. The first crease in the palm starts on the right side beneath the little finger and it typically stops before reaching the palm's left side. The next crease down is the opposite; it starts on the left side of the palm near the thumb and index finger and stretches across the palm. It fades before it reaches the other side. Approximately in the center of these two creases, in a direct line from the index fingertip, is a spot where the proximal phalanx ends and connects to the metacarpal palm bone. This is the metacarpophalangeal joint. Aikidoists referred to this bone as the yonkyo spot, and it is used to apply pressure point pain.

Push into the palm a bit and you will feel this spot, a bony protuberance. Flex your knuckles forward and this bone will become even more pronounced. When applying the yonkyo pin, this is the correct position of this hand, and it cuts into the sensitive areas on the inside of the attacker's wrist. The right-hand provides additional control, and once this grip is attained, no matter what the previous attack had been, the defender extends forward with his or her entire body, and then cuts down as though cutting with a sword. As previously explained, it is a mistake to focus on applying pressure point pain. Such pressure will be there, but focusing on that will make your technique weak. Instead, keep in mind the following guidelines:

1. Make sure that you are moving with your entire body. Do not just move your hands and arms to affect the opponent.

2. Keep your shoulders down and in place, and do not try to muscle the opponent. If you are moving your entire body as one, you will have control. If you are only moving your hands or arms, the technique's application will be reduced to a contest of strength.

3. Do not try to control the opponent's arm or wrist, and do not try to cause excessive pressure point pain. Instead, try to instantly take his balance as the technique's application begins, thereby controlling his entire structure. This is the key to all Aikido techniques.

Practitioners who have been training for years are often able to apply this technique with no pain whatsoever. When uke attacks, nage unbalances and controls his entire body, and nage does not need to enhance or highlight the pressure point control. Nevertheless, when students begin practicing Aikido they do not yet have such skills, so knowing how to target this pressure point and others like it is useful, if not necessary knowledge. The human body has many pressure points, and some can be targeted in the same way as a standard yonkyo technique, making use of the same hand position.

> "If you are surrounded by a host of enemies or if you need to protect others from enemies who wish to cause them harm, realize that you may actually have to maim or kill."

Targeting Pressure Points

These spots include the back of the wrist as opposed to the inside, and the inside of the ankle. Nage can target such places with other body parts, such as the knee, elbow, foot, and big toe. Practitioners can discover such applications after leaving the dojo, by thinking about the techniques they learned that day and how they might apply them in unusual situations in which they are on the ground or being attacked in unorthodox ways. With a little bit of imagination, a ton of practice, and some serious thinking, dedicated Aikido practitioners will know how to apply a variety of pressure point techniques while on the ground or in other seemingly disadvantageous positions.

All the human body's pressure points can also be targeted with strikes, and there are many of them. Such points are located along the body's main arteries and nerve centers, but all joints are also good targets. Many pressure points are targeted for health benefits in acupressure and acupuncture. The same points, when attacked, can cause serious injuries or worse, so it is important to understand what reactions each strike will elicit, and to never strike training partners in such places. Knowledge of the points and how to target them is an important part of any martial art, but Aikido is not destructive. It has been called an art of peace. In a sense, this moniker has given many people the wrong idea, and they think that Aikido is not a martial art, but more of a spiritual discipline completely removed from techniques of attack and defense. That is not what the founder intended.

The art he created contains dangerous techniques and in his own words "powerful strikes that can kill." But O-Sensei perceived a larger purpose. Having served in the infantry in the Russo-Japanese War, and having seen his friends and students die in the horrors of World War II, he devoted himself to harmony. He said, "A warrior receives the gift of life and establishes life everywhere; love is life, the essence of the divine plan." He also said, "Aiki – the wellspring of love's power: make the glory of that love ever increase!" His spiritual focus does not mean that he disregarded martially viable attacks and defenses. On the contrary, he recognized that such techniques were necessary to dispel evil and protect the innocent. Aikido practitioners who strive to understand the founder's art must learn how to kill and control people, and yet they must choose not to.

With this in mind, learn how to defend yourself in any possible situation. If you are surrounded by a host of enemies or if you need to protect others from enemies who wish to cause them harm, realize that you may actually have to maim or kill. Striking pressure points can cause such results. Some major pressure points targeted in martial arts are the temple (*kasumi*), the throat (*chikake*), solar plexus (*suigetsu*), and spots above, below, and to the side of the nipples (*myo*). To see just how painful such points are, and to find the correct

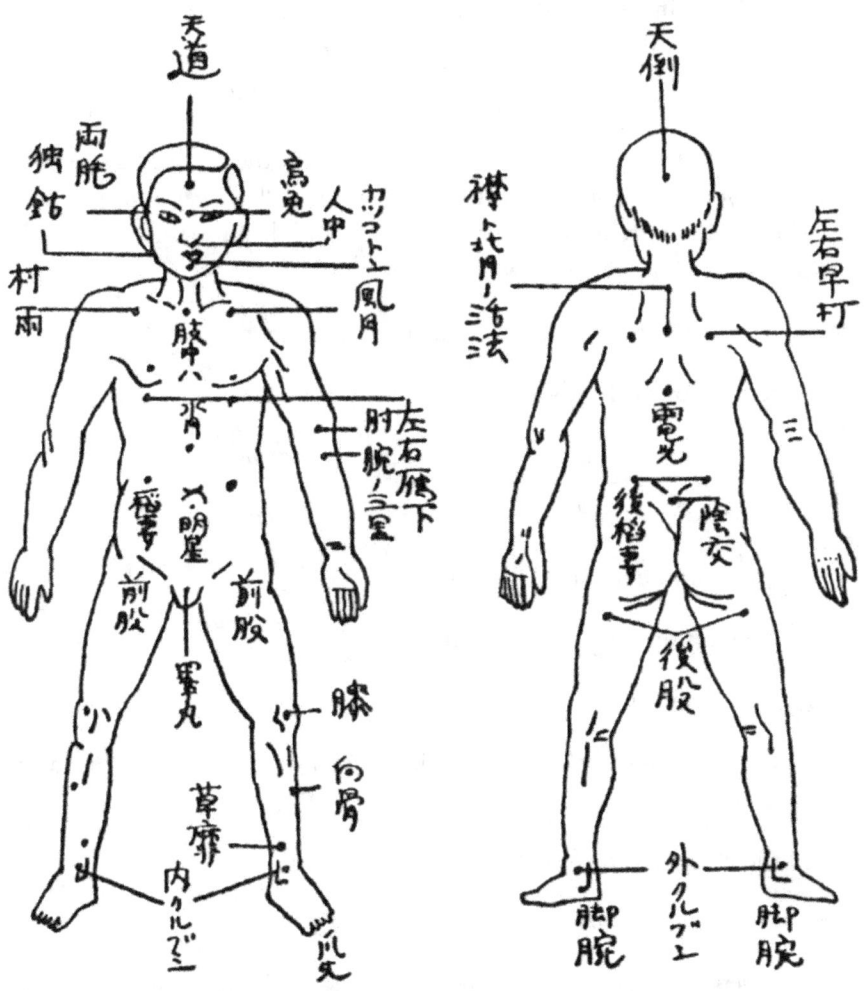

Pressure Point Locations (front)
Credit: Image is in the public domain Source: These two images were retrieved from http://www.progettomarziale.com/?page_id=91. They are also found at http://www.depasqualejujitsu.com/history/jujutsu_files/sekiguchiryu/sekiguchiryu.htm

Pressure Point Locations (back)
Credit: Image is in the public domain. Source: These two images were retrieved from http://www.progettomarziale.com/?page_id=91. They are also found at http://www.depasqualejujitsu.com/history/jujutsu_files/sekiguchiryu/sekiguchiryu.htm

spots, push in with your fingers. Find a place approximately an inch above or below your nipple and push it. You will discover a tender spot that causes pain. Then, starting at the nipple again, move your finger to the side of your body until you hit a point where your chest muscle meets your ribs. At this spot, push in again. If you don't feel an intense pain, you are in the wrong place. Move your fingers around until you find the correct point, and once you do, figure out how to target that spot on others. You will not be pushing in, but striking the point, most likely by making a fist with the knuckle of the middle finger raised, and using this knuckle to target the small pressure point (*nakayubi ipponken*). You could also move your middle finger on top of your index finger with both of the fingertips aligned, and then use this to target the same pressure point (*nihon nukite*).

Other pressure points include the following locations:

1. the top of the head (*tendo*)
2. a spot between the second and third rib (*denkosuei*)
3. just underneath the mastoid process (*dokkusumi*)
4. a spot in the inner thigh (*kansetsu*)
5. the edge of the rib cage (*getsuei*)
6. the side of the wrist (*horyu*)
7. the tender area behind the ear in which the jawbone attaches to the skull (*dokko*)
8. the elbow joint (*shitsu*)
9. the scrotum (*tsurigane*)

The Japanese words for such pressure points are not the same words used for these body parts. Such terms are specific to the pressure points themselves. Again, use your fingers to find such points on yourself, and then determine where they are on others and how to target them. Do not strike others to find them.

When targeting such points, you may need to use seemingly unusual hand positions; these lead to strikes that are common in other arts but typically not taught in Aikido, such as the hiraken (fig. 2.1), spear hand, two-finger spear hand, palm-heel strike (fig. 2.2), and the nakayubi ipponken and nihon nukete strikes previously described. Depending on the pressure point's location and size, different types of atemi must be used. The shuto or tegatana is useful for

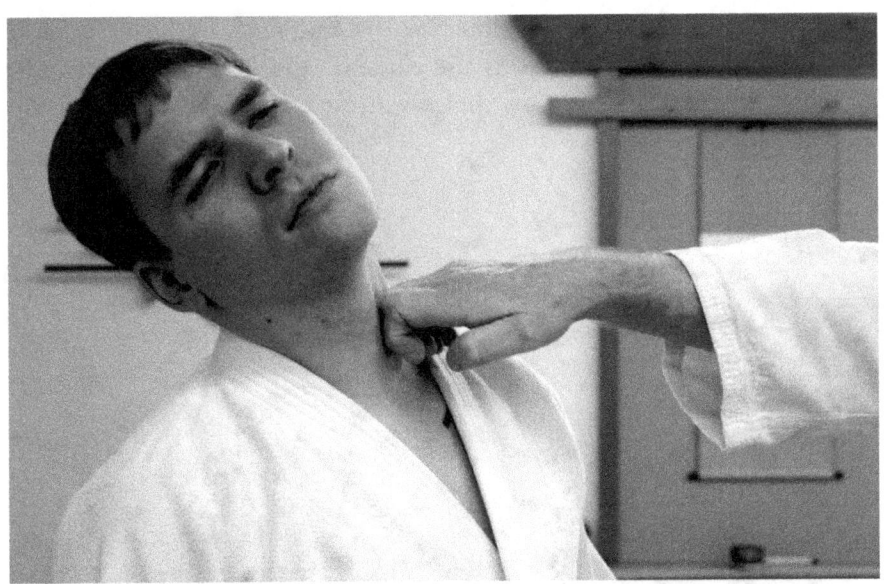

2.1 Use a variety of strikes to target diverse anatomical weak points, such as this hiraken.

2.2 A palm-heel strike can devastate targets like the chin.

certain *kyusho* (pressure points) along the attacker's neck, as shown in figure 2.3. Using the thumb (fig. 2.4) is also efficient. Just keep in mind that the attacking direction and weapon choice will force uke to react in different ways.

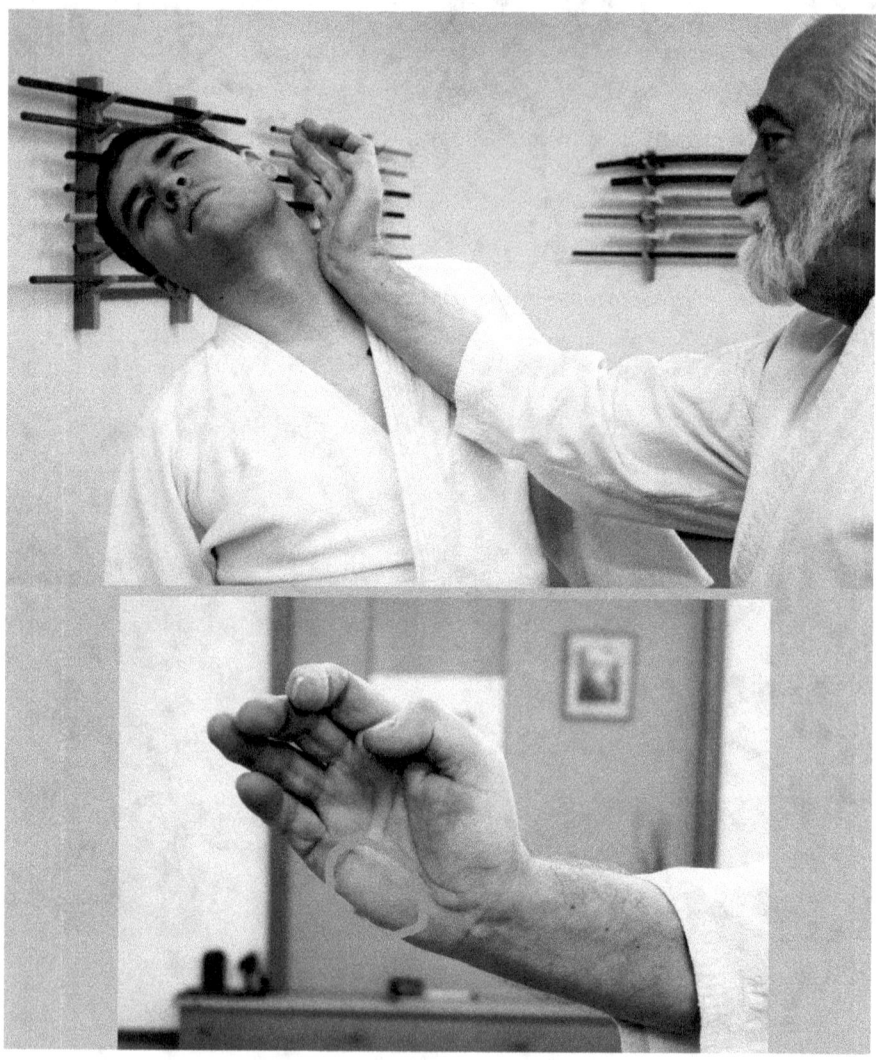

2.3 Proper training in shomenuchi can help students to effectively use the shuto.

Beyond using hands and fingers, consider other body parts that can target pressure points, such as the elbow, knee, the heel, and (if it has been conditioned) the big toe. Other body parts may be used in uncommon circumstances, such as while you are on the ground or pinned against a wall. These include the front and back of the head, the shoulder, and anything else you can think of. If you are only accustomed to the standard strikes

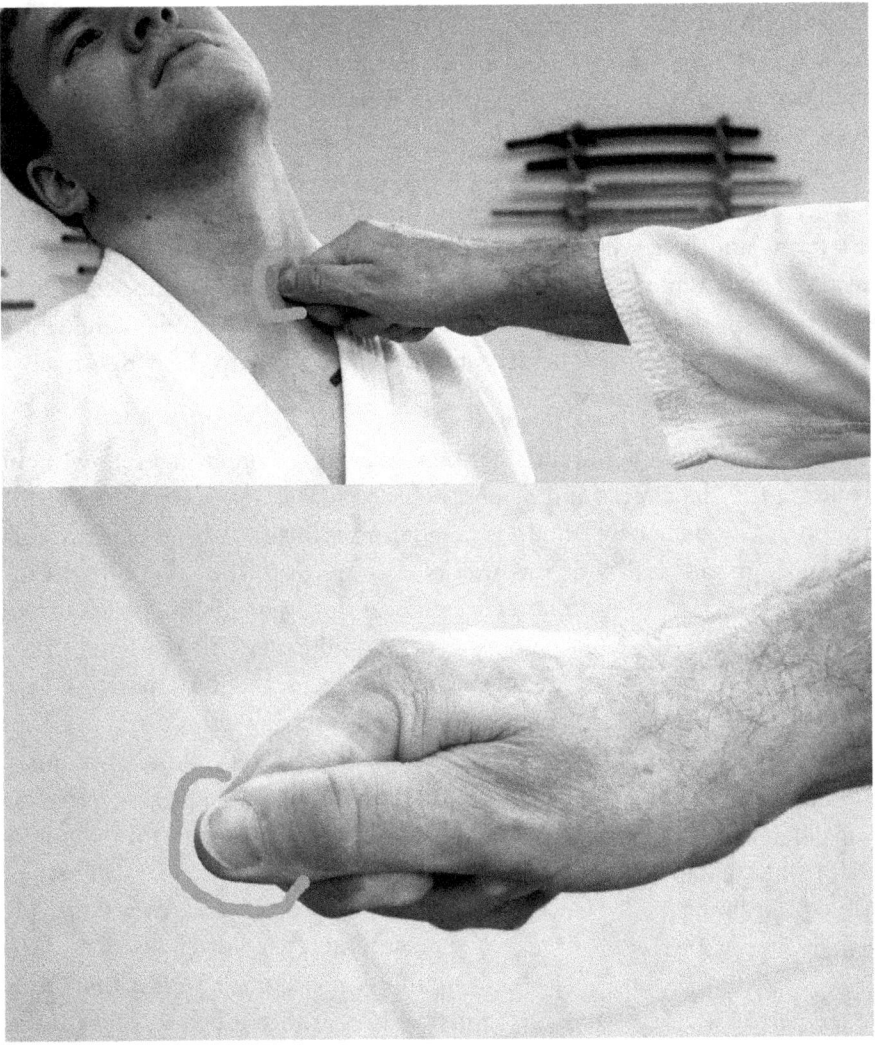

2.4 The thumb can likewise be used to target pressure points.

used in Aikido dojo (tsuki, yokomen, shomenuchi, etc.), which make use of standard hand positions such as a fist or shuto, you will not be prepared for an actual fight. A person's rank does not indicate combat prowess, and many people who have been training for years in arts like Aikido can be defeated by individuals who have never studied a martial art in their lives, but who have grown up fighting.

Moving beyond Form

Consider Musashi Miyamoto (c. 1584-1645). From what is known about him, he was not a formal student of any martial art, and yet today he is considered one of the greatest Japanese swordsmen to have ever lived. He reportedly killed many accomplished martial artists. He wrote about the martial arts, including the famous *Book of Five Rings* and the lesser-known *Way of Walking Alone*. Reviewing his texts, it becomes clear that he despised set forms and believed many martial arts schools include flashy or showy techniques that might look nice but are ineffective in actual combat. William Scott Wilson explained this: "[Musashi] declared that if students relied on such techniques, it would be the same as fighting only to die with attractive form, but without victory."[22]

Some students training in different martial arts get caught in a trap without realizing it. The attacks and defenses trained in the dojo are not necessarily realistic. Consider how Aikido is taught and trained. A beginner can walk into a dojo and deal with the attacks that are thrown at him. It doesn't matter if he moves slowly, he can be successful and he will not be injured. This is a good thing. People must feel safe and supported if they are to continue down this path. But after five or ten years of this kind of training, that beginning student is no longer a beginner. Nevertheless, they continue to defend against the same types of attacks and defenses. After years, the practitioner has gotten used to such training and doesn't realize that he is unable to deal with more realistic attacks. This is because he is surrounded by a

> "Some students training in different martial arts get caught in a trap without realizing it."

Musashi Miyamoto (c. 1584-1645)
Credit: Image is in the public domain. Source: Retrieved from https://en.wikipedia.org/wiki/Miyamoto_Musashi#/media/File:Musashi_ts_pic

particular training and teaching method and no longer realizes that anything is lacking. He has become, as Sagawa Yukiyoshi said, "Like a frog trapped in a well."

For the frog, the well is his life. It is everything he knows, and he does not realize that there is an entire world outside it. To get a black belt in some modern martial arts, one only needs to keep showing up at the dojo and paying for tests; however, the color of one's belt is worthless and has nothing to do with martial capabilities. To truly progress from beginner to expert, students must broaden their horizons. They must consider all sorts of attacks. They must figure out the principle beneath the form, and they must do what O-Sensei modeled: they have to move beyond set forms. He said, "Aikido has no form; it is the study of the spirit." He also said, "In Aikido there are no forms and no patterns. Natural movements are the movements of Aikido. Its depth is profound and it is inexhaustible."[24] The founder's son, Ueshiba Kisshomaru, explained this statement:

> "The meaning of the founder's statement, frequently spoken in his personal, esoteric style, may not always be clear. For beginning students intent on mastering the different forms and techniques, his statement contradicts everything they are taught. If Aikido has no forms or patterns, what is the use of learning the different techniques? What is meant by natural movements? Can I move any way I want to? The first thing to note is that the founder's statement is not meant for beginners but for advanced students. It is advice directed to those who've attained a certain level of proficiency and yet are still so attached to form that they lack the natural, flowing movements that are the ultimate manifestation of Aikido. In a real sense, his words are meant to encourage advanced students to work harder until they attain the goal of Aikido. A classic Japanese proverb says, "Enter by form, and exit from form.""[25]

This kind of advancement takes real effort, real thought. It is easy to show up at the dojo and go through the motions, just continuing to do what you have done year after year. And if you are only training in Aikido or other arts for exercise or social interaction, this is okay. However, if you wish to defend yourself or others with Aikido, you must figure out how Aikido techniques can work in unusual situations. Learn how to strike correctly and with power, not just using your hands or feet, but other body parts. Learn how to target pressure points, and then figure out how to use strikes in any technique without interrupting the flow. Practitioners will find this hard to do because it is difficult to take a step back and view their own training as an outsider would.

It is like the scene in *The Matrix* in which Keanu Reeves has to choose between the blue or red pill. If he chooses the blue one, he goes on living the only life he has ever known, but if he chooses the red one, the world he recognizes collapses, and he is unable to deny the scary truth of existence. This might seem like an unusual analogy, but it is apt. Take your Aikido outside the safe dojo. Talk to a friend who boxes or practices a different martial art. Then get together and experiment. It doesn't have to be confrontational or scary, and it can be fun and enlightening. Find out what works and what doesn't, then strive to make all your Aikido techniques work, keeping in mind the founder's admonition that Aikido has no set form. Also keep in mind Musashi's hatred for showy techniques, things that look good but might not work. Do not worry about what your techniques look like or the fact that they are different from the techniques trained at the dojo. Just stay true to each technique's principles and make them work. Whether they are applied in a grappling situation on the ground or with strikes instead of pins, you can remain true to Aikido principles and be successful in real situations. This skill will not develop on its own. It takes an open mind, dedication, and persistence. These qualities and this kind of training will make you skillful.

> "The color of one's belt is worthless and has nothing to do with martial capabilities."

3

STRIKING IN AIKIDO: THROWING TECHNIQUES

Just as atemi can facilitate gaining control of an attacker, which leads to a submission, strikes can also be useful in throws. In some cases, a properly timed atemi can break your partner's balance, thus moving him into a position in which he no longer can adequately defend himself. Alternately, a strong atemi at the correct angle could actually *become* what seems to be a throw. In reality, it is not a throw, just a strike that sends the attacker rolling across the mat or forces him to land on his head near the defender's feet. Keep in mind that it is not possible to take ukemi from such strikes, however, and do not ever train in this manner because someone could become seriously injured. Train safely, but just learn to see the infinite opportunities to cause real damage in the techniques you already know. To explore this further, let's take a brief look at some of Aikido's throwing techniques, and at how atemi make such waza viable.

Kaiten-nage

Kaiten is the Japanese word for revolution or rotation, so kaiten-nage is best translated as "rotary throw." Like all previously described techniques, it can be performed no matter what the attack is, but it would be difficult to use on someone who did not dedicate himself to the attack. Considering that a skilled fighter is not going to put all his energy into a single attack, it is tough to demonstrate this technique as a logical

"The color of one's belt is worthless and has nothing to do with martial capabilities."

3.1 Consider all the potential strikes that become available in a technique like kaiten-nage. (uke Ryan Kashmitter)

3.2 Nage unbalances uke and then strikes naturally based upon his stance and motion.

conclusion to a punch or thrust with a weapon. This is how it is typically trained in dojo: the attacker will lunge forward with a punch. Assume it is the right one. Nage enters the attack and simultaneously steps off the line to the left while turning his own body to face the opposite direction. At the same time, his shuto intercepts the attacking arm just above the elbow (fig. 3.6). Blending with the attacking movement, he continues uke's motion forward and slightly across the body before cutting down toward the ground. When he cuts down, he put energy into it, which brings uke's head down.

At this point, the defender moves his right hand to the back of uke's head in the same manner in which he would issue a shomen strike. The left hand never loses contact with the attacker's right arm, and, as the defender's right hand moves to the attacker's head, his left hand moves around the arm and grasps it in the wrist area. At this point, the attacker's head is down low, and his arm is high. Maintaining this pressure, the defender directs the opponent's arm along an angle across his back, and he steps forward to execute the throw. Beginners often practice this technique because it gives them an opportunity to practice their ukemi skills as well as other competencies considered important in Aikido: breaking the opponent's balance while maintaining their own

3.3 Nage strikes uke with his elbow, thus halting his movement and making some time and space (maai).

3.4 Many other strikes can be used in this and other techniques, all of which unbalance the attacker in diverse ways.

balance, and never meeting force with force. It is a great training technique, and it would work in a realistic situation if an angry attacker came at you with everything he had, throwing a so-called haymaker. However, someone who actually knows how to defend himself would not do such a thing. He would strive to stay centered, and a single punch would be followed by many others.

Think about the combinations that boxers practice. Assume that you are dealing with someone who knows how to cause damage with his hands. When he jabs, you might have to parry and then jab yourself. You have to bait him. Make him think you are unprotected in certain areas, which you want him to attack. This consideration is foremost when a martial arts practitioner has a sword in his hands. He thinks about it all the time. When the sword is over his head in jodan, it makes the attacker want to strike low; when he drops his swords to gedan, this position makes the opponent want to attack high. O-Sensei often took a sword off the rack when explaining key points. Consider what is done with the sword and try to incorporate the same strategy into your empty-handed method of attack and defense. If you play with your combative spacing (maai), even while facing a boxer or someone who fights using a similar style, it is possible to be just outside of his

3.5 Nage issues a backfist to the face to buy some time.

3.6 A strike to the elbow leads naturally into many techniques including yonkyo, or in this case, kaiten-nage.

comfortable reach. In other words, he could hit you, but to do so without stepping, he would have to shift his weight forward. Certainly this is not an easy skill to obtain, but the more you train, the more you will recognize and control maai.

However you do it, your aim is to get the attacker to reach out with one of his strikes (i.e. to overextend), as shown in figure 3.2. When he does so, you can parry the strike with one hand and strike his arm, shoulder or even his head with the other. This same type of entry has been explained with regard to both sankyo and yonkyo. If you can get the attacker's energy moving forward, you can break his balance in the same direction with a properly placed atemi. Then, you can transition into a technique like yonkyo, or in this case, kaiten-nage. If you are able to cut down on the arm to make his head drop forward and down, the technique becomes simple to apply. The entrance (irimi) into the technique (i.e. making or exploiting a weakness) is the most difficult thing, and this is true no matter what technique is practiced. Unfortunately, in many dojo people spend their time practicing the techniques themselves while disregarding the most difficult part to do correctly. It would be far better for practitioners to spend their time working on parrying and entering

3.7 The strike takes uke's balance, causing him to lean forward.

3.8 If the attacker resists the technique, defender can kick his ribs to regain control.

into attacks and moving their bodies in beneficial ways, from which they can deal with such strikes. Knowing how to complete the formal pins of Aikido and other related martial arts is useless if students can never apply such techniques to an opponent attacking realistically. Practice dealing with such attacks at speed. Such training will benefit you and make you a more formidable opponent.

When you have intercepted the incoming attack, perhaps using a strike to continue his movement forward (fig. 3.6), strike down hard with shuto (3.12) as the opponent's head dips. Then, slide your hand to the back of his head so he cannot stand up and regain his balance (3.9). If you need to, you can kick his side in the same manner described in the previous sections on ikkyo, nikkyo, sankyo, and yonkyo. (Remember that all of these techniques build off the first one, ikkyo, and ikkyo is the Aikido equivalent of Daito-ryu Aikijujutsu's ippondori, which contains a kick to the ribs before the concluding pin is applied.) Your opponent is in a compromised position, and if you issue a front ball kick to his ribs, they will likely break, and you will have caused serious damage. If this is not a matter of life and death as you perceive it, and if you have not noticed the presence of other attackers, a true

3.9 Nage strikes the back of uke's neck with shuto.

3.10 The technique begins as a natural movement initiated by atemi.

Aikido practitioner should not do this. Instead, kick his ribs with a left instep kick, (assuming that you have your right hand on the back of his head and are controlling his right arm with your left hand), as demonstrated in fig. 3.8. (It is also possible to kick his stomach or ribs.) As soon as this kick makes contact, do not withdraw it. Continue it forward as though it were a step. Bend that front knee as it moves through the opponent's space while simultaneously straightening your back knee, yet be careful you do not shift your weight onto the front leg. Remain centered. At every moment in this technique, think of what would occur if the opponent suddenly regained his balance and tried to take your balance. In fact, this is a great thing to practice in your dojo no matter the technique.

> "Make him think you are unprotected in certain areas, which you want him to attack."

3.11 Nage throws uke by stepping forward. An added kick could be used if required.

Practice in slow motion and stop at various points. Ask uke to test your balance. He should be able to push or pull you from any direction and you should be stable. The tendency at this point of the technique, whether you include a kick or not, is to shift your weight onto the front foot. This must be avoided. Your weight must be centered. Although it will be discussed in further detail in the final section of this text, one of the basic practices that O-Sensei passed on to modern-day practitioners is an exercise called *funakogi undo*: the so-called boat-rowing exercise that is at the core of some Aikido movements. This exercise causes outsiders who don't understand its purpose

3.12 A tegatana to the back of uke's neck will subdue him and keep the technique flowing. (uke Lucas Brown)

3.13 A knee to the head can also be extremely effective, and it does not interrupt the technique's flow.

to wonder, "What is wrong with those Aikido people? They're pretending to row boats!"

Think of how this exercise is practiced. Using their entire bodies as one, students move their hands to their center and then unleash power forward, and when the two motions are joined and done repeatedly, it resembles moving with oars to power a boat forward. Done correctly, students should always be balanced and centered. Their weight never shifts to the front or back foot as they perform this exercise. Anytime something moves forward, something else has to move back and vice versa. Keep this in mind when performing kaiten-nage. You are controlling his head with your right hand while you have his arm above his head and across his back, and you just issued a kick to the underside of his ribs. This will be shocking for him but will not cause unnecessary damage. Keep your energy moving forward, the entire body moving as one, and turn the kick into a huge step. Your body weight will be behind it, and so will your energy. Be sure that your left arm does not collapse as you do this. Keep it straight and power through, making sure you do not lose control of your own balance. Always keep your center.

> "O-Sensei stressed the importance of being able to defend oneself from all directions, and part of this is being able to throw an attacker in any direction."

Done correctly, you will have thrown the opponent. This technique is used when you want to make space, and when you don't want the opponent next to you at the conclusion of your movement. The more you practice this technique and consider options for the inclusion of atemi, the more proficient you will become at its use. Keep in mind that the direction of the throw can be modified. Once the technique has been applied, you can throw the opponent in any direction. It won't actually feel like a throw. It will feel more like a shove or push, but in all respects, it is a throw (nage). Consider how striking applications will change depending on the throw's desired direction. For example, kicking his right hip facilitates the ura version. Many other possibilities exist. O-Sensei stressed the importance of being able to defend oneself from all directions, and part of this is being able to throw an attacker in any direction. He specifically included shiho-nage as one of Aikido's pillars to likely teach this concept.

Shiho-nage

Many photographs of O-Sensei show him with a sword, and in videos and photographs alike he is seen cutting in the four cardinal directions before he begins teaching. An ardent follower of Omoto-kyo, this was originally a practice called *shiho-hai*, showing reverence to divinities in four directions. With the sword, this action is even more efficacious, as a sword is symbolic of cutting through delusions. Many of the Buddhist Guardian Kings hold swords, such as Acalanatha (Fudo Myoo), Trailokyavijaya (Gosanze Myoo), Yamantaka (Dai-itoko Myoo), Vajrayaksha (Kongoyasha Myoo), and Atavaka (Daigensui Myoo). Their swords cut through delusions and falsehood, giving practitioners a clear glimpse at reality and helping him or her along the path toward enlightenment. When martial art practitioners pick up a sword and cut in the four cardinal directions, it is called *shiho-giri*. In Aikido, the same spiritual idea is manifested with empty hands, and it is called shiho-nage: four-direction throw.

> "Aikido techniques are used to control the opponent and move him in any direction."

Throwing in Four Directions

First, let's discuss the basics. Your opponent grabs your left wrist with his right hand. You are facing north, while uke faces south. Step with your left foot, setting it down across from yet just outside of the opponent's right foot. Energize the fingertips of your left hand and drop your elbow, thus removing slack from uke's arm. Grab the inside of his wrist with your right palm, making use of the base of the index finger's proximal phalanx. It should be directly over the pressure point targeted in yonkyo, only in this application the attacker's arm and therefore wrist are positioned differently.

Fudo-myoo and others carry symbolic swords.
Credit: Photo use courtesy of Sailko, made available as part of the Wikimedia Creative Commons. Source: https://commons.wikimedia.org/wiki/File:Periodo_heian,_fudo_myoo,_XII_sec

3.15 Consider all the striking possibilities in shiho-nage.

3.16 Uke attacks with yokomen, and nage strikes his face.

Maintain the taut feeling in uke's arm and pivot on your left foot, bringing your right leg around so that you are facing the direction in which you started. You move under the opponent's arm, but do not raise his arm up. Keep it on a horizontal plane as you pivot. Once you are facing the opposite direction and your left foot is forward, pivot again, this time keeping both feet planted. At the conclusion of this movement, you are facing the same direction as when you started. Cut down on the opponent's arm, causing him to be thrown to the north. This is the technique's ura version.

From the same starting position, remove the slack from the attacker's arm and add your right hand. At the same time, step in and across your opponent (at an oblique angle) with your right foot. This step should be in the northeast direction. Then move your left foot to the northwest and turn. Remove your left hand from his grip, add it to the back of his hand in a position just below your right hand, and cut down as though you were cutting with a sword, thereby throwing him to the south. Next is the western throw. You are going to change your stance from the initial starting position so you end up in right hanmi facing east. Move your left foot first, followed by the right. Then, go through the exact same motions as the previous two throws. Make sure

3.17 The strike leads naturally into the technique.

3.18 Strike uke's ribs with your left fist and then continue to move his arm across his body.

3.19 Step across uke's front. Use your left elbow to strike his ribs. Then turn, keeping his arm low.

3.20 Holding his wrist and hand with both hands, cut down as though cutting with a sword. If he struggles, use atemi to take his balance and regain control.

that you have removed the slack and throughout the throw make sure his arm remains extended, as this is the only way you can maintain control without returning his balance. For this particular throw, once you have assumed a stance with your right foot forward, slide that right foot in. Then step with your left, turn, and cut down. This is the standard omote version.

The last of the shiho-nage throws will obviously send your opponent to the east. Similar to the previous technique, change your stance by stepping out with your left foot. Next, step in deeply with the right foot at an oblique angle across your opponent's center. It is possible to

3.21 If uke resists as you cut down, sweep his right leg with your right leg. Think of it more like a kick to his lower calf and it will work better.

skip the very first step, that of changing stances, and instead begin with this deep right step. It depends upon your relative body sizes, the amount of slack he has in his arm, and the power of the grab itself. If you can remove slack and establish a tautness without stepping to the left, do so. Extraneous movements should be eliminated as much as possible.

Once you step in and across with the right foot in a large motion, step in the opposite direction with the left foot. It will feel like you are stepping behind the attacker, and you are once again stepping toward the northwest. Finally, turn so that you are in a right hanmi, and adjust your grip and throw as though you were executing a shomen sword cut. These are the four variations of shiho-nage practiced in dojo across the world, but sometimes shiho-giri (four-direction

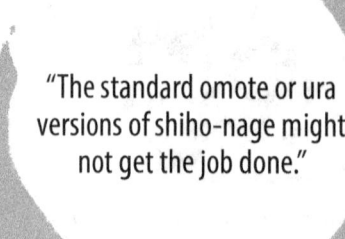

"The standard omote or ura versions of shiho-nage might not get the job done."

3.22 The technique's conclusion. Do not get caught up with the pin, as uke could shift positions and attempt to thwart your efforts. This could lead to a grappling situation on the ground.

cuts) becomes happo-giri (eight-direction cuts), and this can be done empty-handed as well.

Turning Four Directions into All Directions

Aikido techniques are used to control the opponent and move him in any direction. Practitioners simply need to become talented enough with the technical applications themselves so that the modifications needed to move an opponent in a different direction are natural. Eventually, they will not require thought. If a second attacker approaches, you can maneuver the first attacker in such a way that he protects you from the oncoming attack. Either that, or you might need to move the opponent to prevent a serious injury from occurring to him. If an angry or intoxicated person attacks you near a staircase or railing, it is up to you as an Aikido practitioner to control him and keep him safe. The standard omote or ura versions of shiho-nage might not get the job done, and maybe the other two directions aren't enough either. By changing your footwork you can change the throw's direction. The more you practice this technique, the better you will become at its use, just like everything else in life. It only takes time and dedication.

Shiho-nage and the Sword

Instructors often teach shiho-nage with a sword, as it highlights essential movements and the technique's feeling. When someone raises a sword over his head to strike, nage steps into and across the attacker, slitting open uke's stomach as he passes through. Then, while his left foot is forward, he turns and delivers the coup de grace, cutting off the opponent's head. This is the shiho-nage throw to the south. A minor variation alone is needed for the

O-Sensei demonstrates shiho-nage Credit: From the collection of W.G. von Krenner

throw to the west, and a completely different approach is required when demonstrating the ura version. Typically, the instructor parries the incoming attack with his sword and then pivots on his left foot, moving his body completely around with the *tenkan taisabaki* movement that Aikido consistently reinforces. Then he turns and cuts the attacker's neck. Although the maai with swords is larger than required by this technique's empty-handed version, the body movement is the same.

> "In many traditional martial arts and modern arts like Aikido ... students are expected to watch technical demonstrations carefully and then steal the techniques."

Anyone who really knows how to use a sword would most likely be horrified by these movements because this is not the manner in which a Japanese katana is efficiently used. Using the sword only demonstrates the correct body movements, and students can follow such movements better when grabs and throws are removed. For advanced practitioners, such a tactic is unnecessary because they have already learned how to watch techniques to gain knowledge and proficiency. In many traditional martial arts and modern arts like Aikido, which have adopted some traditional characteristics, students are expected to watch technical demonstrations carefully and then steal the techniques. If they did not see the small shift in the feet or the subtle control initiated by the hara, it is their loss. This is truly how instructors of East Asian arts thought. However, this attention to detail, this kind of vision is not easily developed. Sit a bunch of beginners down and show the technique without any explanation and you will see just how lost they can be. In fact, try it as an experiment. Then, after noting the ensuing disaster as they begin practicing it, stop the class, demonstrate the same movement with a sword, and then have them practice that. You will see that they can follow along more easily. This is because the movements are larger, the angles are highlighted, and they are no longer focused on "putting a technique on someone," which clouds their vision. Do not think of the sword movements in a martial sense; if you ever did this to someone who knows how to hold a sword, they would kill you. Instead, consider it a teaching mechanism alone. There is a simple reason such a mechanism is used: it is effective.

Strikes and Shiho-nage

Shiho-nage will work well against untrained opponents, perhaps a drunken patron in a bar or even a bouncer, but it will be difficult to apply to someone trained to fight, such as a grappler or boxer. The reason this technique and many others in Aikido work is because you are moving the opponent's arm in an unnatural position across his own body. A fighter is going to avoid this at all costs, so as you begin applying shiho-nage, he will move his own body, change the angle you are trying to affect in his arm, and play with the energy you are providing to remain in a safe position. Nevertheless, if your opponent extends his arms to grab you, or if you're already in a grappling situation and they become available, there are opportunities to apply this technique. As evidence of this fact, similar techniques exist in almost every jujutsu style. One technical change can be implemented to make this technique more effective in a realistic situation. Typically, once both hands are applied to your opponent's attacking arm, those hands are together: your right hand touching your left or your left touching your right. If they are not exactly touching, they are close enough that they appear to be in contact with one another. Instead, move your lower hand to his elbow.

> "Always feel as though you are extending energy from the fingertips and even the elbow joint."

If he attacks with his right hand, move into the standard shiho-nage technique, blending in the same manner with your right hand grasping his right wrist, drawn across his body. As soon as possible, apply your left hand with the fingers up to the outside of his elbow joint. Apply pressure as you continue to twist the arm with the right hand (and body behind it), further compromising the elbow joint's position with your left hand. When performing this variation, be sure that you do not collapse your left arm. You do not want the arm to remain stiff, but you don't want it to collapse as the opponent attacks. Always feel as though you are extending energy from the fingertips and even the elbow joint. In time, and with enough practice, this will prevent your arm from collapsing. Now, let's take this a step further. If you practice this variation in your respective dojo, you will see that it opens an entire realm of striking possibilities. First, instead of your left hand going to his elbow and then applying pressure, that hand could issue a potentially bout-changing strike to the outside of his elbow joint. Instead of pushing, strike. Then, follow it up with more atemi.

Depending upon how the opponent is moving, when you strike the outside of his elbow joint, his head might move closer to you. If so, his right temple might be an appropriate place to strike next. If it is not necessary to cause damage, yet you doubt the ability to complete the technique without another strike, strike the side of his face instead. Then continue applying the pin or throw. If the opponent moves in a different direction after you begin the technique, he is still susceptible to different strikes: to the ribs, side of his neck, or a low kick to the back of his knee or ankle. No matter which you choose, such striking techniques will have a devastating effect on the attacker. Please keep in mind the points that have been highlighted throughout this text so far, especially the most important: make sure that the strikes flow with the technique rather than running counter to it. Atemi can also be a quick fix. If a technique is executed perfectly you might not ever need to use atemi-waza, but human beings are not perfect creatures; we are prone to make mistakes. Therefore, don't be surprised or become overwhelmed when a mistake occurs. Use atemi to set things right! If you mess up a technique and feel the opponent struggle, strike hard and fast and apply any technique that appears. As strange as it might seem, a strike often makes multiple technical conclusions possible. The more you practice this in your dojo, the more you will realize how true it is. Just keep in mind that it is important to practice such techniques safely so no one gets injured. O-Sensei cautioned, "Since all techniques can be lethal, observe the instructor's directions and do not engage in contests of strength."[26]

Effective Practice

Human beings are constantly changing. They never stand still. After years of training we all become conditioned in one way or another, whether we know it or not. Training in any true Budo, a way that combines physical and spiritual paths, is always beneficial, but many stories exist in which a high-ranking martial arts master was defeated by an outsider. In Japanese history there was a practice called *dojo-yaburi*. This term literally means "dojo breaking," and it referred to a regular occurrence. Practitioners of one style would show up at the dojo of another and challenge the top students. If they were victorious, they would have a match with the instructor. And if they beat him, the dojo would be destroyed. Students would leave, perhaps studying under the victors, but no matter what, the style would no longer be respected, and for the most part it would die out. Sometimes, martial artists who were defeated were only defeated because they were too focused on their own style. In other words, they practiced holding a sword and moving in a certain way for so long that they may have become blind to other ways to use it and other ways to move the body.

In modern martial arts, practitioners must prevent a similar thing from occurring. Although practices like dojo-yaburi do not really occur anymore, it is easy to get used to moving in a certain way and not preparing to deal with other arts' practitioners who might move in different yet effective ways. Considering just Aikido, after years of training with cooperative uke, nage are sometimes shocked when a fighter from another style doesn't "go along for the ride." Many Aikido dojo emphasize spiritual aspects, and fighting techniques are not generally practiced because spiritual ideals like joining all human beings together take precedence. If this is what you are after there is nothing wrong with it, but take a critical stance and view your Aikido for what it is. Then, set aside a particular class or two in which you explore what happens when uke moves in an unexpected way. When you first start working on this, you might find that you are mentally focused on completing one particular technique, such as shiho-nage. When uke changes his position, another technique might make more sense, but rather than abandon the initial technique, nage continues trying to apply it. This is because his mind is trapped on that waza. This is not a matter of him being an ineffective practitioner. It instead has to do with his practice.

If you are not sure if this is the case, watch people practicing randori. The first few years, people get stuck using the same technique repeatedly as they are attacked from different directions. To get beginning students through this stage, instructors function as coaches. They make suggestions. They slow it down, and as attackers come, they remind students of techniques that they know how to use. They say shiho-nage, now irimi-nage, etc. In time, students begin to use the various techniques in different orders, depending upon what is most effective based upon each individual attack.

This is a natural and logical progression. It is a training method used to make students' minds more expansive, helping them to see the bigger picture. But we become trapped in other ways. Ask your uke to resist at different portions of the technique by changing his body position. Keep this practice light; do not apply techniques with real force, as people could be seriously injured. Obviously, that is the last thing any Aikido practitioner would want.

Here is the goal: assume that you start applying ikkyo. Uke shifts his body. No matter what, you cannot continue putting ikkyo on him. You must change the technique. Let's say you switch to shiho-nage. Once he changes position again, you must use yet a different technique. And this practice can continue. Don't ever finish a technique; just continue switching from one technique to another. Eventually you will be able to speed up and even add power. This is a useful training method, and it is suggested that individuals serious about their Aikido skills adopt it. It will release your mind, and after training this drill routinely, you will not be stuck on any particular technique. This leads to both bodily and mental freedom, which opens the door to unlimited techniques. There is no end to your potential. Train in this manner and you will begin to see things anew. You will see possibilities that were previously obscured, including technical variations: the energy changes when one technique flows into another, and countless opportunities to apply atemi-waza.

> "Human beings are constantly changing. They never stand still."

Sumi-otoshi

First, for readers unfamiliar with what this technique looks like, let's begin with a grabbing attack: katate-dori. Uke steps in and grasps your left wrist or forearm with his left hand (fig. 3.25). Step out and to the right with your right foot while simultaneously extending your right arm down and forward (figs. 3.28-3.29). Rather than do it physically, which could result in stiff arms among beginners, consider the energy inherent within your body. Extend energy through your fingertips while keeping your arm and body relaxed. If you are new to Aikido and other similar Japanese or Chinese arts, this may seem unusual or even impossible, but the more you train the more you will come to feel and use this energy.

There is a common Aikido exercise in which students place their arms on partners' shoulders, and then their partners apply pressure to the inside of the elbow. Beginning students are generally instructed to resist using muscular force at first, just so they can feel such stiffness. Then, they are asked to relax the arm completely, and to feel as though the arm were a fire hose filled with water rushing out the fingertips. The more pressure is applied to the elbow, the more that student should relax and experience this energy. This is a basic exercise designed to teach students there is power in relaxation, and such power is superior to muscular strength. Tohei Sensei said that this was the most important concept that O-Sensei taught him. Thinking students (i.e. students who do not just show up at class and go through the motions) will spend years exploring this concept and improving such skills. The more it is trained, the stronger it gets. This topic will be explained more fully in the final section of this book (jodan), but for now, consider the feeling of ki flowing through your arm and out your fingertips.

3.24 The basic version of sumi-otoshi begins with a katate-dori grasp.

3.25 Nage instantly breaks uke's balance

 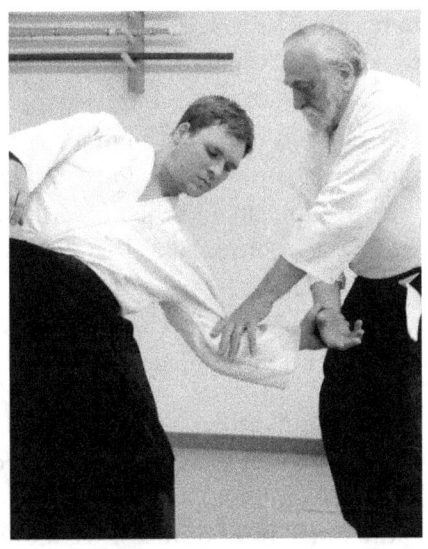

3.26 The left hand is applied to the inside of uke's elbow.

3.27 Uke's balance is broken in many ways, but it is important to always remove the slack and then take his center.

Step out and to the right with your right leg leading, extending energy down and away from the attacker. This will remove the slack from his arm, and it may shift his weight to his left side. This is the desired effect, although in an actual combat situation it will be difficult to achieve. But in the dojo, we perform two-person kata (forms), taking the roles of uke and tori, and kata are important for teaching forms and principles alike. Explore the balance breaking process. As you move, make sure you stay in balance, constantly remaining centered, with the goal of upsetting your training partner's balance. Once the slack is removed, turn slightly to your left, step in and behind the attacker while simultaneously applying your left hand to the inside of his elbow joint (fig. 3.27-3.28). Make sure that your arm does not collapse. You need to keep it extended. However, do not tense the arm muscles. As previously mentioned, think about relaxing the arm (and body) and extending energy. This will get the job done.

With your hand on his elbow joint, apply pressure downward and across his back. In other words, do not push his arm away from his body or straight down, as this will have no effect on the opponent. Here is a good practice activity: after the first step and unbalancing movement, stop. Ask your partner to remain where he is; in other words, he does not shift his weight or posture to regain his strength. However, using beginner's style (muscular) strength, he should resist the technique's application. When you push straight down, you will find that the technique is ineffective. If you push in other random directions, you will see similar results. A common beginners' tendency is to raise the arm up and then scoop down. This occurs because nage wants to see uke do a break-fall. They find it fun. However, a break-fall should not be considered. Instead, find the angle that works and engrain it. Make it second nature. The technique works only when you disrupt uke's balance in a downward direction across his back.

Now that this aspect of sumi-otoshi has been understood, let's continue on to more important aspects of it. This technique, the way it is typically practiced in an Aikido dojo, can only work if the attacker remains unbalanced the entire time. It is not that he cannot strike you throughout the technique; he can, but if he is off balance, he cannot generate any real power, so you do not have to worry. However, it is difficult to take someone's balance and then keep him unbalanced. As soon as uke feels his balance being compromised, he will correct it to protect himself. As an interesting side note, this natural

3.28 In reality, a strike can take his balance more easily.

3.29 Striking variation. The preemptive strike prevents uke from striking.

3.30 Even if uke blocks the strike, nage will have forced a reaction, thus leading to uke's defeat.

human tendency is what makes some of the Daito-ryu Aikijujutsu "sticky" techniques work. Practitioners move the opponent into a compromised place and then rest them against an outside object (often their own bodies), from which they seem trapped. For example, using one technique, nage grabs both of uke's forearms and rotates them in a manner similar to shiho-nage. He turns at the same time, until uke and nage are back-to-back. Uke's hands are placed on nage's chest, and he moves forward, which seems to trap uke. He feels like he cannot move.[27] People experiencing this technique are only trapped because they are trying to regain their balance; they are trying to stand up straight. It is interesting that the way out of such techniques runs counter to that natural human tendency.

Since human beings wish to stay balanced, sumi otoshi would be difficult to apply to non-compliant uke. When performing sumi-otoshi, strikes can help to cover your mistakes. After the first step to the left in the previously described kata, strike (figs. 3.29-3.31). Again, think about where you want to strike to facilitate the technique. Sumi-otoshi will send him back and to the ground. Therefore, a strike to the stomach will move his body into a disadvantageous position. One to the jaw or nose will have the opposite effect. It will further disrupt his balance in the direction in which you want him to move. Such a strike complements the technique rather than disrupting it. This is an important point that readers must take away from the beginner's section of this book (shodan).

Martial Variation

Before moving ahead, let's take sumi-otoshi a step further. This technique, even with strikes that cover weaknesses and disrupt the opponent's posture, is impossible against a skilled opponent. As with all techniques, the principle behind it must be considered before practitioners can adequately use sumi-otoshi effectively in a realistic situation. This is not an easy thing to do, and it marks the difference between beginners and advanced practitioners. Considering traditional sword arts, kata can be performed in public, but the real techniques are not displayed. The real attacks and defenses are there, so practitioners who know the hidden teachings can improve their skills, but beginners who have learned the outer form alone are blind to the real killing moves, which require different targeting, a change in maai, or other minor adjustments. Such minor adjustments change how one sees not only kata, but fighting in general. Even though Aikido is a modern martial art, not associated with samurai in the least, it is thought that O-Sensei based its techniques and teachings on old styles. If this is the case, the real techniques are there, hidden in kata. To find the real sumi-otoshi, let's look at a martial variation of the technique, and then the Judo version, which was one of the original 40 throws that Kano Jigoro included in the Kodokan Judo curriculum.

The opponent attacks with a right punch. It doesn't matter if it is a straight punch or a roundhouse, and it is unimportant if you are standing in *shizentai* (natural posture) or a particular hanmi. Think *irimi* (entering) as you step in deeply with your left foot. Do not be afraid of the attack. A common error in this variation is to step out and away. Do not do this. Step in! Meet the attacking arm with your left palm. When this contact occurs, your own hand should be close to your face. Experiment with this feeling. A large movement is not required to get off the attacking line. The step directly forward with your left foot and a slight body turn is enough. Practice this until it becomes comfortable. If you are a beginner or if you are nervous, ask your training partner to slow down. Make it safe while perfecting the movement. Once you are comfortable entering into the attack and meeting it with your left hand, it is time to consider the right arm.

"Remain centered and concentrate on moving from your center, the "hara" as it is known in Japanese."

Your right hand and arm should be extended on the inside of the opponent's attacking arm. In other words, his attacking arm separates both of your arms. Think of it like an X-block found in most karate styles. In such arts, it is often thought of as an arm break, the defender's two arms functioning not as blocks but strikes. When the attack comes in, the defender strikes the inside of the forearm with his right shuto, and he strikes just above the outside of the elbow with his left palm. In sumi-otoshi, it is a similar idea, but the arm position is different. In the Aikido version (provided it was a right-sided attack), the left arm is on the outside of the arm, and its relative placement does not matter. The right arm extends and makes contact with the inside of the attacker's elbow. Once this contact occurs, continue forward and apply pressure in the same direction practiced in the standard version of this technique. Do not try to throw the opponent, and do not use force. The harder he attacks, the harder he will hit the ground, but you do not need to alter your motion.

For the most part, you will not need to step with your right foot after springing in with the left. The throw will already have been completed. However, he might change his strike, and perhaps it was even a feint. Stepping in with your right foot will help to maintain the connection between attacker and defender, and if he changes his body position, this connection will allow you to adjust and possibly gain the advantage. Therefore, think of this technique as a standard sumi-otoshi. All Aikido techniques have throwing and pinning variations. If you take his balance gently and then step forward with your right foot, you will unbalance him to the rear. Instead of letting him hit the ground, you can keep him on his feet. From this position, in which his weight is pulling him backward toward the ground, you can keep him up yet unbalanced. It can function as a come-along, albeit an unusual one, or you can apply any number of concluding pins. Practice this technique and play around with its many variations. It will help you understand the underlying principle of sumi-otoshi, and this understanding will then influence your approach to the art itself.

To further such comprehension, let's take a quick look at the Judo version of this same technique. Judo's sumi-otoshi is a hand throw. Assume you have grasped the opponent's right sleeve with your left hand and his upper lapel (the left chest area of his keiko gi) with your right. When uke steps forward or when you are able to force him to shift his weight to his left side, step in deeply with the left foot while pulling down and back with your left hand. The right hand, driven by the right elbow, forces uke in the same direction. Once his feet are in the air, use the hands and arms to drop him to the ground, where a ground pinning technique (*newaza*) can be used. Judo's uki-otoshi (floating drop) is in all respects the same technique as sumi-otoshi, but uke is thrown forward rather than back. If he overextends forward, this motion can be continued by turning in the same direction as uke: in essence blending with his movement. Then cut forward and down with the left hand and up and forward with the right hand.

Both of these techniques are often seen in Aikido randori, and they are typically just referred to as kokyu-nage. (Many unnamed techniques in Aikido are often thrown into this category. This is not appropriate, as kokyu means breathing, and kokyu-ho refers to breathing and meditative practices. It may be useful to adopt some terms used in Judo or jujutsu styles to distinguish between such techniques.) Consider both sumi-otoshi and uki-otoshi as they are performed in Judo. Practice such techniques, as they are certainly part of Aikido. Then, practice the martial version of Aikido's sumi-otoshi as

Uki-otoshi variation

described above. Finally, return to the kata form typically practiced in dojo. Once you consider all facets of this technique, the kata will make more sense.

When training this and all other Aikido techniques, learn to sense and feel changes in your partner's balance. Pay attention to your own center, and work hard to never give it up. Remain centered and concentrate on moving from your center, the "hara" as it is known in Japanese. It is much more difficult that many think it is. Do not perform techniques quickly. Go slowly and really experience the movement. Are you balanced and rooted the entire time? Where are the technique's weaknesses? How can you cover such weaknesses to protect yourself? Will a punch or kick do the trick? If so, where and when should you strike? All such considerations will help to make you a more formidable practitioner, and discovering the truth about techniques can really only be done in slow motion.

Taijiquan practitioners perform their *tailu* (forms) in incredibly slow motion. They work to make their movements flow, one change blending seamlessly into the next. Then, they work to connect breathing to movements, and finally, they concentrate on *neigong* (internal exercises) to develop *jin* (internal power). Such training is high level, and performing forms slowly is the key to progress. Aikido practitioners can learn much from *taijiquan*. Sure it is fun to throw quickly, and it may function as a workout or stress reliever. But for real progress, take your time, think, and really strive to uncover the base principles that make this and all other techniques work. Such training will eventually pay off.

4

PUTTING IT ALL TOGETHER

The techniques explained in the previous sections are limited examples of the many applications in which atemi can be useful or even necessary. However, it is important to never *plan* to do a technique. If you get caught up with a particular technique, you will likely be defeated. Instead, when an opponent attacks, use correct body movements to respond and attack at the same time. After proper tai sabaki, striking opportunities emerge. Most atemi serve the same purpose, with the exception of preemptive strikes and those that function as irimi, which will be dealt with in the next section. To eliminate the common beginner's dilemma of *trying* to do a particular technique, don't do them at all. Focus instead on specific attacks, responsive and correct body motions, and then atemi. Disregard the techniques themselves, and you will find that opportunities to employ such waza appear. Atemi makes them easier to apply. The following pictures will give you some idea of the variety of striking possibilities, which creates time and space:

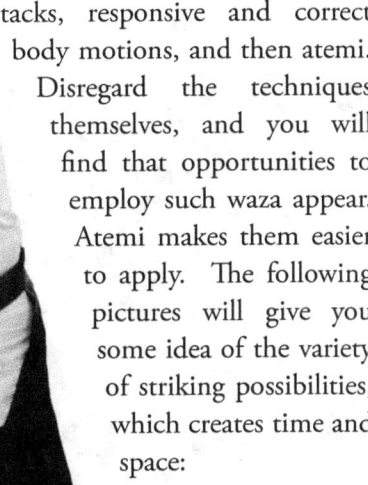

Striking Sequence from Katatedori

4.1

4.2

4.3

4.4

Striking Possibilities from a Straight Punch

4.5

4.6

4.7

4.8

From Empty-handed Shomenuchi

4.9

4.10

4.11

4.12

From Shomenuchi with a Sword

4.13

4.14

4.15

4.16

From Yokomen Attacks

4.17

4.18

4.19

4.20

From a Round-house Punch

4.21

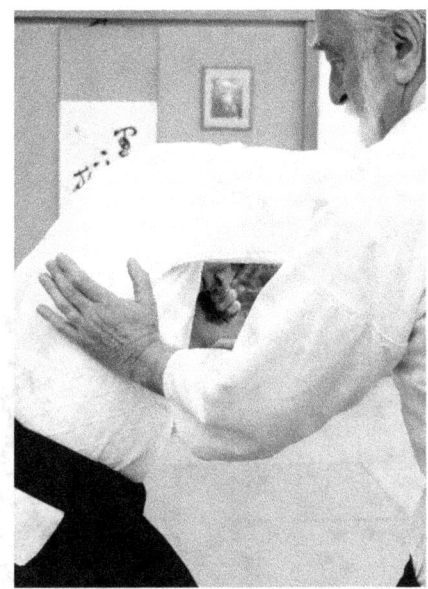
4.22

4.23

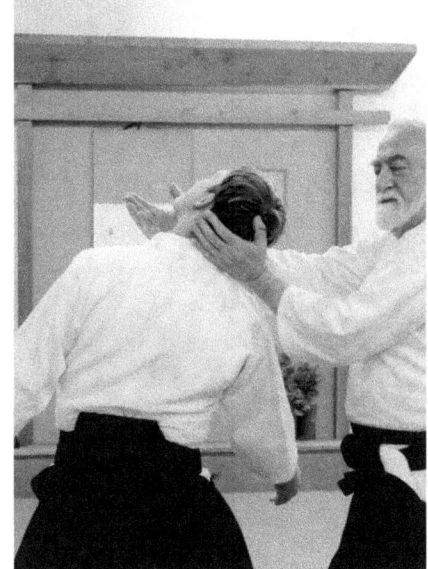
4.24

Possible Entries and Strikes for Kicks

4.25

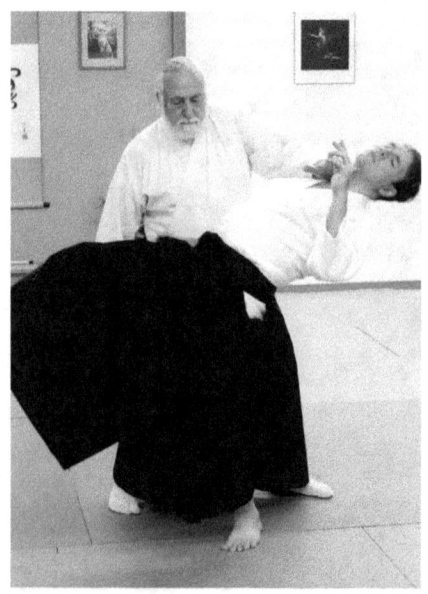

4.26

4.27

From Grabbing Attacks

4.28

4.29

4.30

4.31

From Grabbing Attacks *continued*

4.32

4.33

From Grabbing *continued*

4.34

4.35

4.36

Knife or Club Attacks

4.37

4.38

4.39

After any one of the previously demonstrated initial blends, use whatever atemi are available and logical. You could strike to the neck, as shown in figures 4.17, 4.18, and 4.19, or to the ribs, like in figures 4.21, 4.22, 4.33, or 4.37. If you are grabbed from behind or in another unusual manner, strike the attacker's groin with either your fist (fig. 4.31) or with a knee (fig. 4.28). Likewise, when the opponent kicks, strike his groin (4.27), his throat (4.25), or use the strike to blend directly into a technique, such as that shown in figure 4.26. While the left hand strikes the neck and then remains there to control the head, the right hand can be used to sweep the attacker's right leg off the ground. This will plant uke onto the ground. If a maiming technique were required, nage could simultaneously drop onto one knee, bringing the opponent's back on top of his braced upper leg, thus breaking his back. Such a technique is found in Aikido's parent art, but a safer and perhaps more ethical version is typically trained in Aikido dojo: one in which the attacker can actually take ukemi to protect himself. In many real techniques, no ukemi is possible. Generally, use whatever body parts are accessible and logical when striking. It is advisable to hit hard targets with soft parts of your hand, and to hit soft targets with the body's hard parts, such as elbows, knuckles, knees, etc.

The previous examples, and others like them, can also be seen in the book *Budo*, which O-Sensei wrote. It was published by Kodansha, and it contains numerous photographs of him using the correct body motion to get out of the way while simultaneously striking. It also has explanations of how to perform certain techniques, and pictures clearly demonstrate that he used atemi at the techniques' onsets, throughout their execution, and at their conclusions. Like most books about Budo, his aim was not to teach a person unfamiliar with the art. Instead, it supplements the instruction and training of serious practitioners. Teachers and advanced students do not need a technical, step-by-step book of instruction; instead they can use the photographs and explanations to delve a bit deeper into the art that they study. By doing so, they can begin to comprehend those underlying secrets that many never discover.

Aikido's founder stated repeatedly that a large part of any technique is atemi. Unfortunately, the way some people perform Aikido today is completely useless and ineffective because they lack understanding of atemi's true purpose. A flutter of the hand is not atemi. It must be real and focused.

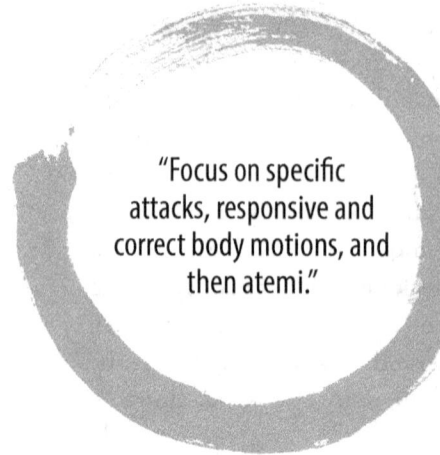

"Focus on specific attacks, responsive and correct body motions, and then atemi."

It should not have a built in intention like, "I am not going to hit." An attack that is not meant to actually attack and damage is (obviously) not a real attack! Atemi should be focused. It must do its job! At the last moment, the strike can be stopped to protect your training partner, but it has to be real from the beginning. This takes precision and control, and it will help your partner learn how to protect himself from strikes. Such concepts will be explored more fully in the next sections of this text.

There are critics out there who do not think Aikido is a viable martial art. Strangely, such critics even include some high-ranking Aikido teachers, who do not like to think about striking or ground techniques or any real technical applications. So many photographs of Ueshiba clearly show him striking. After training in Aikido for more than 55 years, and training in Japan at the Hombu dojo while O-Sensei was still alive and teaching, I can say with certainty that modern Aikido is not what the founder taught. It is hoped that students delve into their martial studies and learn how Aikido's techniques can be used in real situations. It might look different and it might not be pretty, but O-Sensei had real martial skills. He could strike powerfully and he could defend himself from the ground using techniques that he referred to as Aikido. The purpose of this book is to help earnest practitioners add such striking techniques to their Aikido repertoire, just as the point of our previous book was to help them to apply techniques that they already know to a grappling situation on the ground.

Other Techniques

We have received a great deal of positive feedback regarding our previous book *Aikido Ground Fighting*. We are happy that it has affected how Aikidoka train, and that it has caused many to see Aikido with fresh eyes. One criticism was that the book does not contain many techniques (outside Aikido's curriculum) even though it was about ground techniques (which some believe do not exist in Aikido). The purpose of the text was not to supply readers with new techniques that one can use while grappling. In fact, doing such a thing would not be right (in our opinion). The founder had a vision, and if people are going to train in an art called Aikido (his art), they should follow his lead. He selected a small number of techniques from the hundreds of techniques in Daito-ryu Aikijujutsu, and the techniques he selected were not the most lethal jujutsu variations. If the art he developed focused on self-defense alone, he would likely have picked different techniques, as there are some vicious bone-breaking, maiming, and killing methods within the complex art. But this was not his purpose. He picked techniques that would physically represent the spiritual concepts of the Omoto-kyo religion, and techniques that would embody the sacred sounds adopted from Indian indigenous religious beliefs; these were called kotodama in Japanese.[28]

Striking or Ground Techniques: The Same Mentality

Aikido's limited techniques demonstrate unlimited potential. In *Aikido Ground Fighting*, we attempted to demonstrate that one could end up on the ground in many ways while using Aikido techniques. When you do ikkyo

4.40 *Maintain a martial approach. Consider all aspects, all potentialities. (uke Ken McCaskill)*

to someone, he or she might roll out of it. With nikkyo, he or she might go to the ground, speed up to change the trapped arm's angle, and then roll out again, using the feet to kick your head on the way. If you are not ready for such a scenario, you will be defeated. If you sense it occurring and are able to defend yourself, you could end up in a grappling bout on the ground. And if you have never trained to deal with a grappler, you will be defeated.

If you want to learn great grappling techniques, study an art that specializes in them like Brazilian Jujutsu. Such techniques are not found in Aikido. However, if practitioners never consider what to do on the ground, there is an inherent weakness in the way they train. If you consider the principles of Aikido techniques rather than how they look or how they are performed from a standing posture, you can apply them anywhere. We provided some basic techniques, variations of which are found in Judo, because those particular techniques blend well with standard Aikido techniques. In addition, newaza's purpose in other arts is to pin a person on the ground or to gain an advantageous position from which one can strike. That is not its aim in Aikido. Its role is to temporarily control an opponent (using what Aikido practitioners already know), so they can safely rise to suwari (kneeling) posture. Practitioners move around on their knees while practicing pins and throws. From such stances, they can drop to a prone position on the ground or spring to their feet.

> "True skill emerges just by considering Aikido's techniques in a more expansive way."

While performing suwari-waza (also known as *zaho*), practitioners can apply techniques or make space, into which they can safely rise to a standing posture. Thinking of it this way, a large number of techniques is unnecessary; true skill emerges just by considering Aikido's techniques in a more expansive way. It involves thinking outside the box, and considering the art anew. This is the only thing students need to do to keep Aikido fun and interesting. Otherwise, in time, techniques lose their luster. They become boring, and as years progress, people stop coming to the dojo, thinking they have gained all they can from Aikido. In ancient times, studying a martial art involved loss, not gain. The time needed to commit to an art took practitioners away from school and family, and they embraced an austere lifestyle. Consider this. Are you willing to dedicate yourself to the art? If so, try to see it from an outsider's perspective. Find its strengths, consider its weaknesses. Then, figure out how the art's preexisting techniques can be used to cover such holes. If O-Sensei were ever caught off guard and taken to the ground, there is no doubt he would have been able to defend himself. And he would likely have called any technique that he used Aikido, because he claimed that "Aikido has no techniques."

Reviewing the first portion of this text, some readers might wonder why more techniques were not covered. Certainly, there are more techniques that could

4.41 Train to strike with many different body parts, and learn how uke responds. Then, make sure that the strikes are logical with regard to the technique's flow.

be explained, with striking opportunities, etc., but the point is not to spell out how atemi-waza fits into every technique that you know. It is an attempt to open people's eyes about the effectiveness of techniques that you practice, and the countless variations possible. Such variations emerge while focusing on the underlying principles rather than the technical form. Using the examples provided, consider where and how a variety of strikes can be added to your techniques. Note that many body parts can be used to strike, and depending on the circumstances, some will be effective and others ineffective.

Use your feet, heels, knees, elbows, fists, shuto, fingers, and more. Learn to spot and attack sensitive areas. Then, make sure that you understand how uke will react upon being struck. Will he move into a weakened position, or will he become stronger after having been struck? For example, if he is already bent over at the waist, and you knee him or punch him in the face, you will stand him back up, returning his balance. Such a strike is therefore illogical. Finally, make sure that the strikes you use do not interfere with the techniques' flow. The more you consider such opportunities, the better you will get. Train hard and train smart. A thorough understanding of such technical principles and their countless variations will lead one from the beginning level of Aikido to the intermediate and advanced levels.

PART II. CHUDAN (INTERMEDIATE) LEVEL: IRIMI

Isshun no fui uchi (A moment's hesitation will decide your fate).
Calligraphy by Walther G. von Krenner

5

IRIMI AND OTHER CONCEPTS FROM SWORD ARTS

The principle of irimi exists in all Aikido techniques, as it exists in all martial arts. Performed correctly, it is nage's initial movement when dealing with an attack. Generally classified as go-no-sen, movement in response to an attack, it still dominates. If nage initiates the attack, he cuts the opponent down by entering. In go-no-sen, he does not step off the attacking line. He enters it and takes the advantage. Once broken, the opponent can be led around with ease. Thus, even a turning tenkan movement, for which Aikido is known, can only be competently performed if irimi is present first. To understand this concept more fully and its inherent relationship to atemi-waza, looking at the concept in sword arts is useful.

Ono-ha Itto-ryu is an art that Takeda Sokaku studied at the Yokikan Dojo. He was primarily a swordsman, and the principles he learned with a blade affected the techniques passed down through the Takeda clan in Kai Province: techniques that he would later assemble in a new art called Daito-ryu. Therefore, by looking at this sword art's teachings, we can gain direct insight into the nature of Aikido and Daito-ryu principles. Ono-ha Itto-ryu was founded by Ono Jiroemon Tadaaki (1565-1628), who was Ito Ittosai Kagehisa's successor. Ono fought a duel with another student and emerged victorious, so the art was passed along to him. He even

> "The first movement is not a strike, nor is it any real attack. It is only a movement that will reveal potential strengths and weaknesses."

instructed two Japanese shogun. Today the art is still extant, and students of other ryu praise and study its principles.

Shisha Tachi

Three of its principles are of note, since they are seen in the empty-hand arts of Daito-ryu Aikijujutsu and Aikido alike. The first is called *shisha tachi*. Shisha is a Japanese term meaning "scout." Before an army advanced, the scouts were sent out to assess the opponent. In a similar way the kissaki (sword tip) is used to lure the opponent, to make him react and move, so nage can gain insight into his skill and the way he moves his body and weapon. Thus, the first movement is not a strike, nor is it any real attack. It is only a movement that will reveal potential strengths and weaknesses. In a fight, an opponent will react to multiple fast jabs. His reaction may reveal a weakness. Perhaps he drops his guard or raises it to high, or maybe he issues a repetitive counterstrike. No matter what, the initial movements (i.e. jabs) were scouting movements, which provide information.

Makura no Osae

Another is *makura no osae*, which translates to "pillow pin." The real meaning of osae outside the martial arts is to push or hold (down), hence the osae-waza techniques in Aikido and other arts. This relates to a technique in Daito-ryu Aikijujutsu that practitioners usually refer to as "paintbrush." It has this name because the arm moves as though it were painting a wall or fence, with the elbow leading the movement. This common yet high-level teaching is seen in many if not all Daito-ryu techniques, and this skill has led to discussions about elbow-power in both Aikido and its parent art. Makura no osae is also found in other sword arts, such as Musashi Miyamoto's (1584-1645) *Nitenryu*. In his *Book of Five Rings*, which is divided into four sections, Ground, Water, Fire, and Void, he discusses "holding down a pillow" in Fire. He writes:

> ""To Hold Down a Pillow" means not allowing the enemy's head to rise. In contests of strategy it is bad to be led about by the enemy. You must always be able to lead the enemy about. Obviously, the enemy will also be thinking of doing this, but he cannot forestall you if you do not allow him

to come out. In strategy, you must stop the enemy as he attempts to cut; you must push down his thrust, and throw off his hold when he tries to grapple. This is the meaning of "to hold down a pillow." When you have grasped this principle, whatever the enemy tries to bring about in the fight you will see in advance and suppress it. The spirit is to check his attack at the syllable at..., when he jumps check his jump at the syllable ju..., and check his cut at cu... The important thing in strategy is to suppress the enemy's useful actions but allow his useless actions. However, doing this alone is defensive. First, you must act according to the Way, suppressing the enemy's techniques, foiling his plans and thence command him directly. When you can do this, you will be a master of strategy. You must train well and research holding down a pillow."[29]

> "The study of Aikido and other high-level martial arts takes decades. Every technique contains multiple layers of understanding."

Shimabukuro Masayuki (1948-2012) described this common technique further in an article entitled *Principles from Ono-ha Itto-ryu*:

> "This [...] refers to the principle of restraining or holding an opponent with the light touch of a pillow. This principle can be demonstrated in the example of someone sitting in a chair and then attempting to stand up. Typically, one feels very strong when they rise. But a light touch of the finger to the forehead of someone sitting in a chair can prevent them from rising. In practice, if one applies *osae* when the opponent cuts or thrusts, one can immobilize the opponent, preventing him from applying a technique. The application of *makura no osae* requires correct timing as well as the ability to read the opponent's intent."[30]

O-Sensei pointed out that his techniques came from the sword, and since Takeda considered himself primarily a swordsman, the same can be said about the techniques of Daito-ryu Aikijujutsu. If you square off with an opponent and always consider that you are holding a sword (or that your shuto are swords), you will see how sword techniques apply to empty-hand movements. The key to performing such pillow sword movements lies in the elbows' directive power. Such power is typically tested and displayed using *Aiki sage* or *Aiki age*, so in Aikido it is seen in *suwari-waza kokyu ho* and other techniques like *tenchi-nage*. However, the principles manifest in all techniques. The most powerful and important principles, like the elbows' use and the concept of irimi, are difficult to develop. It takes years to begin to understand how to perform such movements, to recognize them in all techniques, and then to apply them. For this reason, the study of Aikido and other high-level martial arts takes decades. Every technique contains multiple layers of understanding. It is for this reason that irimi-nage has been called the ten-year-technique, meaning it takes more than a decade to do correctly. Many beginners would find this statement perplexing, because they might think that they can do it correctly after only a year or two.

> "In one movement, you receive the opponent's attack, displace it, and then cut him."

Isshin Itto

Irimi is another overarching principle of the art Takeda Sokaku studied, Ono-ha Itto-ryu. They call it *isshin itto* (one spirit or heart, one sword). The word shin is pronounced kokoro when it is written alone, and this word can translate to either heart, spirit or mind. It is in reality a concept that combines the three of these, one that does not exist in English. Soseki Natsume (1867-1916) entitled one of his books *Kokoro*, and it was later translated into English as *The Heart of Things*. Hopefully, this brief explanation will provide readers with a better understanding of isshin itto's meaning. It is irimi, and it is best summed up by this statement: "two swords cannot occupy the same space, so I will take that space."

In one movement, you receive the opponent's attack, displace it, and then cut him. You do not move off the attack line. Nor do you cut along the attacking line. You cut through the same line, entering completely. This is irimi. In Itto-ryu, the attacker's sword is displaced by the *shinogi* (the sword's ridge line), which makes his cut ineffective. As you cut through his cut, the cutting motion turns instantaneously into a thrust to the throat (or to the side of the neck if your opponent were wearing armor). This is certainly not an easy technique to master. It is one of the more difficult, yet it is the first technique that practitioners learn in Ono-ha Itto-ryu. Likewise, the first technique in both the Daito-ryu Aikijujutsu Hiden Mokuroku and the Aikido curriculum are the same. Called "ippondori" in Daito-ryu and "ikkyo" in Aikido, they too should be considered high-level techniques. Irimi is in these and other techniques of both arts. It involves taking the opponent's space through greater timing, body development, and a superior mindset (*kokoro gamae*).[31] There is no intentional displacement of the attack or the attacker. You simply enter, and he is displaced due to your dominance. Ellis Amdur wrote that

Irimi is not to get off the line. It is to enter directly, displacing the opponent's attack. Defense is attack. They are one and the same.

this is the true nature of atemi in Aikido: "Using the body (particularly the limbs) to take space the opponent is trying to occupy."[32]

To perform such a movement correctly, you should think of the concept as it relates to swordsmanship. Besides Ono-ha Itto-ryu, Yagyu Shinkage-ryu concepts have made their way into Aikido. Hikitsuchi Michio (1923-2004) taught O-Sensei this art. Among its teachings are Sho, Chiku, and Bai, which were symbolized by *matsu* (pine), *take* (bamboo), and *ume* (plum). Sho is irimi and represented by the triangle, chiku relates to tenkan and is symbolized by the circle, and bai is osae, epitomized by the square. On occasion, O-Sensei drew these three shapes to instruct students in Aikido's finer points. He also explicitly wrote about them, "Study the teachings of the pine tree, the bamboo, and the plum blossom. The pine is evergreen, firmly rooted, and venerable. The bamboo is strong, resilient, unbreakable. The plum blossom is hardy, fragrant, and elegant." Since a triangle represents irimi, this is the form that one should consider. It is the kissaki, the very tip of a sword blade, directed by the entire body, which does not fear an attack. It does not move off the line, nor does it intentionally do anything to the opponent. It simply enters and takes space, and the opponent is thrown into a compromised situation because of the action. In a real sense, it is as though your entire body has become a blade. It functions like a sword. O-Sensei wrote, "Transform your entire body into a true sword."[33] This idea must be carefully considered so it can be put into practice.

Now that the general idea of irimi has been explained, it would be remiss to not include a description of irimi-nage as performed in most dojo, since some readers who are new to the art might be unfamiliar with the technique. It appears in the next section, and O-Sensei's admonitions for performing this correctly in actual combat follows.

6

IRIMI-NAGE

So far in this text, the same attack has been used when describing and illustrating techniques. This has been done for the readers' ease. Continuing this practice, assume you have your right foot forward and your left foot back, and the opponent steps forward to attack with his right hand. It does not matter if it is a straight thrust, shomen, or some kind of a more rounded punch. The only thing that would change, depending on the specific attack, is the timing and spacing, and both of these terms are referred to collectively as maai in Japanese. However, the technique will be the same. Assume it is shomen. As the attack comes in, time it so you can step directly forward, your left foot coming to rest just outside your opponent's right foot but further (fig. 6.2). In other words, your center will be behind the attacker's center. If you move too late, you will get hit. If you move too early, the opponent will track the movement, change the attack, and you will be unsuccessful.

Proper maai will not be attained overnight. You have to practice repeatedly to refine your spacing and timing. This will take years, so do not be discouraged. You must be patient to succeed at anything in life, and this includes the martial arts. The dojo was originally considered life's training ground. Especially after Tokugawa Ieyasu's (1543-1616) unification and then later during the Edo period (1603-1868), when there was not much use for physical techniques as far as their battlefield use was concerned, students learned ethical and spiritual concepts in dojo. They were expected to then apply them to life in general. Do not rush to gain skills. Just train. It was said that O-Sensei once walked into the dojo and witnessed a student making hundreds of cuts with a *bokuto* (wooden sword). It is reported that he said, "One with ki is better than many without!" In other words, when training maai through a technique like irimi-nage, do it with intent. Make

Irimi-Nage as Performed in Most Dojo (uke Ryan Kashmitter)

6.1

6.2

6.3

6.4

6.5

6.6

6.7

Irimi-Nage

 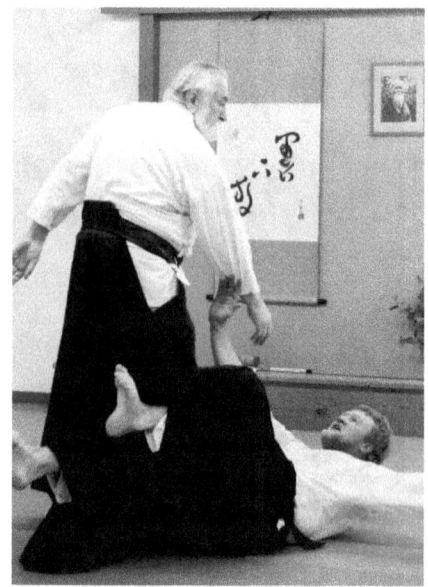

6.8   6.9

your training count. Do not just go through the motions. Really think about what is occurring, and slow down. Move slowly and correctly. Eventually, your maai will improve, and your skills will increase substantially.

Once you step in, turn your center so it faces the attacker. You should always keep uke aligned with your center. In this way, you can use your entire body as one unit, which makes you more powerful. Regarding spacing, you want to be closer rather than further away. If there is too much space between you and the attacker, he can turn and apply jujutsu techniques. With your left hand, control the left-hand side of uke's face and head and move it to your right pectoral muscle, the right-hand side of your chest (figs. 6.3-6.4). Once his head is attached to this spot, your right arm becomes active, and its motion controlled by the elbow (fig. 6.5). Continue moving your arm up and over to break his balance backward (fig. 6.7). At the same time, turn and throw your opponent while stepping in (fig. 6.8). This is one variety. Another is the following: when you enter in the same way, apply your open palm to uke's chin, and then use an added push to carry out the throw. (In a real situation, this would obviously be a strike rather than a push.)

Irimi-Nage Variation

In the book *Budo*, which O-Sensei wrote in 1938, it states that when using this technique in an actual engagement, you must forcefully strike the opponent. At the beginning of the text, there is an explanation of irimi under the heading *training methods*:

> "If you are standing with your left foot forward when the opponent's sword strikes, rely on the principle of kokyu timing to enter smoothly to his side; be prepared to strike a second opponent to the rear with your right hand. In an instant, advance deeply to his back with your left foot, keeping your right foot solidly based, and simultaneously cut down with your left hand to his rear. Step in with your right foot behind him without breaking your posture and down him with both hands."[34]

The term kokyu, as previously mentioned, means *breath*, so thinking of kokyu timing may seem a bit puzzling. However, in some of his waka, O-Sensei elaborated on his conception of the world: one that stemmed from Omoto-

> "This will take years, so do not be discouraged. You must be patient to succeed at anything in life, and this includes the martial arts."

kyo but was uniquely his own. He wrote, "Everything in Heaven and Earth breathes. Breath is the thread that ties creation together. When the myriad variations in the universal breath can be sensed, the individual techniques of the Art of Peace are born."[35] In another passage, he compared breath to the tide's ebb and flow. Therefore, it is safe to assume that his idea of kokyu was more expansive than inhaling and exhaling, although consideration of the breath has always been an important concept in various martial arts.

A basic premise is that one should exhale when attacking, and it is better to attack the opponent when he is inhaling. Beginners and even some advanced practitioners who know how to fight would find this statement a bit amusing because figuring out when someone is breathing in or out would likely lead directly to their downfall. While they try to watch the chest rising or falling, the enemy would attack and they would be defeated. Certainly, doing such a thing is not intelligent. Nevertheless, the breath holds an important place in martial arts, as it does in breath training exercises used for the development of power. When an opponent inhales, his posture changes. Internally, there are changes to the tendon-muscle-fascial chain. The energy it produces can be felt by others. In time, such internal energy can be perceived, as it gives rise to a pattern of movement that is inextricably bound to the breath.

Here is something you should try: using O-Sensei's language, fill yourself with ki and then stretch out your arms. Do not hold any tension in them, but make yourself feel expansive. Extend ki in all directions. Then, inhale and exhale fully as you normally do. When you inhale, the abdomen will expand, and when you exhale it will contract. This is called Buddhist breathing. Now, switch to Daoist or embryonic breathing. In some Chinese styles, this is also called the pre-heaven breath, (and normal breathing is post-heaven). When you inhale, the abdomen contracts and when you exhale it expands. Whether you know it or not, as soon as you begin an activity in which power is needed, like fighting or sports, you switch to this kind of breathing. Keep the feeling of expansive energy emanating in all directions, and feel the changes that take place in your body. Feel the different effects of these two breathing styles, and it will become clear that the breath exerts influence over your bodily tissues. Such an effect is not limited to the amount of air in your lungs. O-Sensei explicitly taught breathing exercises, which he called kokyu-ryoku. These breathing techniques will be explained in the last section of this book. For now, returning to his initial quote, in which the practitioner must enter with kokyu timing, think of the energy flow rather than the breath itself, since they are certainly related.

He then wrote that you should be prepared to strike a second enemy to the rear, and many of his other quotes reveal the importance of being able to deal with opponents coming from all directions. When you really put this mindset into practice, your breathing will change, as will your energy. Tohei Sensei told his students to make themselves as heavy as possible and then extend ki in all directions. This is the same as O-Sensei's statement, "Stay mentally alert in all directions." Do not release your energy toward your opponent, because it will make you weak and unbalanced. You must always keep your center, and being ready for attacks in the four directions (shiho) or the eight directions (happo) is one way to start doing this. O-Sensei also referred to maintaining a six-directional awareness before, during, and after each technique. This particular expression is from Chinese arts, as are many of the exercises and ideas that he passed on. (They will be explored more fully in forthcoming chapters.) O-Sensei wrote, "Functioning harmoniously together, right and left give birth to all techniques. The left hand takes hold of life and death; the right hand controls it. The four limbs of the body are the four pillars of heaven, and manifest the eight directions, *yin* and *yang*, inner and outer."[36] To maintain complete balance and power, and to be able to move in any direction with ease, you must balance yin and yang. If your right hand is yang, your left must be yin and vice versa.

O-Sensei demonstrated irimi-nage in *Budo*. He wrote, "Fill yourself with ki and

> "To maintain complete balance and power, and to be able to move in any direction with ease, you must balance yin and yang."

O-Sensei explained how to correctly perform irimi-nage: with a strong push to the chin, which in combat is a strike with full force. (uke Lucas Brown)

invite your opponent to strike with shomen."[37] After brief instructions for uke, he stated, "Enter to your opponent's right, strike his ribs with your left fist, and use your right [shuto] to cut down his attack. Turn deeply behind your opponent and throw him with the added element of a strong push to the chin." Then, after four pictures that demonstrate this technique, he notes, "In actual combat, strike your opponent's face with full force."[38] In the first picture, he has stepped into his opponent's attack and he is to the attacker's right side.

He is clearly striking uke's right ribs with a left punch as his right hand rides along the attacking arm near the elbow. His centerline faces the opponent, and his balance is centered. In the second picture, he has slid in further behind the opponent, and he has taken control of uke's head and neck. In the third, he turns, adds his right palm to uke's chin, and throws him, and it is clear from the picture that he is using his hips to take uke's balance. Think of how the hips are used in throws like koshi-nage and in Judo-style take-downs like *harai-goshi*, *hane-goshi*, and even *seoi-nage*. The hips serve an important function in just about all techniques, and it doesn't matter if one perceives their use or not. Their additional involvement makes any technique more powerful.

Consider that all parts of your body must be unified. Everything functions together, which makes you more powerful. Perceiving opponents attacking from all directions, extend your energy in all directions. This makes you centered and strong. In time you will become heavier and difficult to move as O-Sensei constantly demonstrated to his students. Use strikes not just to supplement techniques, but as techniques themselves. Irimi-nage is atemi, and atemi-waza is the most important aspect of Aikido, as it will change the attacker's rhythm. It will change how he moves, allowing you to take control.

7

AIKIDO IS 75-PERCENT STRIKES

Atemi in other arts is primarily used to damage or to buy time. Aikido students must learn how to cause injury using strikes in addition to their pinning and throwing techniques, which are trained in a safe manner in a dojo. In a real situation, performed correctly, no ukemi is possible. The techniques will end the engagement, as will powerful strikes that target the body's anatomical weak points. However, for an Aikido practitioner, such study is just background knowledge. He needs to proceed further. Considering the founder's spiritual ideals, and considering irimi's prevalence in all movements, what exactly should atemi do in Aikido?

Its real purpose is to take the attacker's balance. One of the core principles of both Daito-ryu Aikijujutsu and Aikido is kuzushi on contact: instantaneously breaking the balance so uke cannot continue his attack. Consider the irimi-no-ate. As soon as you enter into the attack, taking and controlling space, the opponent cannot continue with his original attack. If the irimi motion is performed correctly, it is probable that the defender will gain complete control of the attacker, thereby ending the engagement. If irimi is not perfect or if the attacker is skillful, it at least stymies his attack and forces him to change his previously intended movement. Ate serves to interrupt uke's intent. Destroy his focus, then move in. But you cannot strike if there is no opening (suki). If the opponent has skill, and he provides no openings, you have to create one. To do this, you must get his mind involved. One way to do this is to move. Consider the Ono-ha Itto-ryu principle of shisha-tachi. Facing an opponent on the battlefield who is wearing armor, you cannot strike him just anywhere. You need to exploit the weaknesses in his armor, stance, and defense. Cuts and thrusts to his armor's gaps is the only logical plan. A strike just beneath the helmet line to the neck, to the leather straps that hold the kote in place on the inside of the wrists and forearms, or to the waist or knees: are logical intended targets: anywhere you can target flesh instead of steel.

If you can find and afford a replica suit of armor, put it on a mannequin that is approximately your size. Then, practice targeting the weak points. If you have never done this before, even if you have been training in various modern-day sword arts (iaido styles), you will find it difficult. Your maai is not perfect, nor is your targeting, but the more you practice it, the better your targeting and distance control will become. A samurai on the battlefield is obviously not going to stand still. He constantly moves, looking to exploit weaknesses in you, all the while striving to keep his own weaknesses covered and protected. Now targeting the armor's weak points is even more difficult. Timing becomes incredibly important. The opponent's movements, meant to kill you, have to be checked and redirected if you are to gain control of the bout. An understanding of shisha-tachi helps. Thrust or cut to make him move. When he moves, an opening appears. Exploit it. The first attack is not the real attack. Swordsmanship consists in one attack followed by multiple others. They never stop. Feints blend with real cuts and thrusts to overpower your adversary.

> "Swordsmanship consists in one attack followed by multiple others. They never stop."

It is important, however, never to use a fake cut or thrust. In other words, there must be intent behind it, and the movement should kill the opponent. If he does not move, he dies. For example, assume that you target the inside of his wrist. You thrust in to cut through the leather and into his flesh, but he pulls his hands up and out of the way. Your motion naturally flows into another cut or thrust which likewise targets his anatomical weak points, such as the armpit or the throat. When he reacts to that (real) cut or thrust, your movement once again naturally blends into the next attack. This does not cease. If you do not have any intent behind the strike, your opponent may recognize this and not react to it. Either that or he may sense your ploy and coax you into a trap he has set, capturing your mind and thereby leading to your death.

A common teaching in many martial arts is to disregard the enemy's insignificant motions and only deal with those that matter. Your opponent will do the same to you. Make sure all your motions are significant, and he will be forced to deal with them. He will adapt to you, which gives you the advantage. Therefore, even though certain movements function as scouts, they *also* are real killing moves. Consider this story about a Chinese martial art expert:

> "Master Lian and his teacher, Professor Cheng Manch'ing, taught in New York City during the early 1960s. On one occasion, a man came to the studio to check out Taijiquan, to see if it could be used for a martial art. It turns out that this man was a Golden Glove boxer. He had asked Cheng if it would be okay to have Taijiquan demonstrated to him. Cheng agreed and told the man to throw some punches at him. The man threw a volley of punches and jabs at Cheng, but all were just feints. After a number of these, Cheng put out his hands and knocked the man down. After getting up, the man was astonished that Cheng knew which particular punch with the real one meant to knock him out. Cheng told him he saw it in his eyes."[39]

Your intent can manifest in other ways, and a skilled adversary will know which attacks are real and which are not. To eliminate this potential weakness, and to cast off unnecessary movements, make all attacks real. Your opponent will sense your intent; he will react and become captured.

Using the Eyes

You have but a split second to capture his mind, and only by capturing his mind can you lead him where you want. One way to do this is with properly placed strikes, which create an opening. Another way to do it is by using the eyes. The mind locks onto what the eyes see. Therefore, we can use the eyes' natural function to trap the mind. Speed is important. If it is too fast, the opponent will not be able to lock onto it, so it will be ineffective. It has to be at a speed that he can follow. If he locks onto a movement, just temporarily, it creates an opening. And although O-Sensei always cautioned students against looking at someone's eyes, as they might intimidate or capture them, Aikido's parent art, Daito-ryu, has the reverse teaching: one should always look into his opponent's eyes, as the eyes reveal his intent. It is believed that O-Sensei cautioned beginners not to do this, but that it is okay for advanced martial artists. O-Sensei himself was known to have a piercing stare, and the same was said about his teacher Takeda. Ueshiba Kisshomaru wrote, "The founder had a powerful effect not just on those direct students who he instructed every day but even on people simply watching his demonstrations or observing classes at the dojo: they say his eyes glittered with a penetration that could pierce metal."[40]

Your intent manifests through the eyes, so you can use your own eyes to move your opponent. It doesn't matter if his movement is a physical, mental or psychological one; it will affect his ki. He will become light on his feet. One way to do this is to look where you want the opponent to look. To properly understand this, forget about martial arts for a moment. If you were in the middle of a crowd at a bus station or somewhere similar, people are on their own paths. They watch out for other people, but they also go where they need to go. Sometimes there are interactions between them; other times there are not. If you stop moving and stare at the ceiling, people around you will start to do the same. They will wonder what you are looking at. That curiosity will cause them to look in the same direction.

Now back to a combat situation: if you break your eye contact with the opponent and seemingly look away, the opponent will do the same. He will wonder what is so important over there. It makes him curious and afraid. Budo is a product of paranoia and fear. People train for self-preservation. If they were fearless, they would not train. This fear dates to prehistoric times, and it has been in our human brains since then. Originally, we were scared of predators, as some species are food while others are predators. This inherent nervousness can be exploited, even by something as

"The mind locks onto what the eyes see. Therefore, we can use the eyes' natural function to trap the mind."

7.1 Nage subtly uses his eyes to distract an opponent. (uke Lucas Brown)

7.2 The distraction causes kuzushi, and it can make the attacker shift his balance and change his attack. This means he is conforming to the defender.

7.3 Once uke conforms to nage, he can be controlled more easily. Using the eyes for this purpose is difficult, and it must be trained for years.

seemingly simple as looking in a certain direction. Curiosity or fear. These things cause him to look, and by looking, an opening appears. Into this opening strikes, throws, or any other techniques can be applied.

Mind Strikes

There are basically two levels of atemi in Aikido and other arts. The first encompasses physical strikes. A study of all their uses could take decades, as it includes where and when to strike, the weapon itself (i.e. fingers, elbows, knees, etc.), and creating or exploiting defensive openings. If this is all you have, you could be a proficient martial artist, but physical strikes alone will spur the creation of counter techniques. If this continues unabated, in years you will have a completely different art. Irimi and its connection to strikes is an important facet, and it will also take years of study to even begin to do correctly. This is not a *level* of atemi, but a principle found in Aikido and all other martial arts, which *connects* to atemi. It requires not just correct body motions, but also a mindset change. Practicing irimi leads to a dominating feeling, and it eventually eliminates the idea of defense. All defensive movements actually become offensive movements, hence the common expression "the best defense is a strong offense." This mindset is developed through irimi. If it is practiced correctly, irimi also can lead to the development of intent, which is a prerequisite for atemi's second level: mind strikes.

This word may sound mystical or magical, but it is nothing like that. The term we are using herein is an artifice, a made-up name to facilitate this phenomenon's discussion. Once you understand it, call it whatever you want. It involves moving with such intent, such force of will, that the opponent reacts to you, whether you make physical contact with him or not. You completely dominate him, and physical contact is unnecessary. A famous Okinawan story illustrates this type of power:

The karate instructor Matsumura entered an engraver's shop in Naha. The shop owner was also an accomplished martial artist, and he challenged his visitor to a bout. Matsumura made a statement about two tigers fighting: one will end up dead, the other maimed. Nevertheless, they both showed up at 5:00 a.m. the next morning in the graveyard of Kimbu Palace, where they faced off. The engraver adopted a fighting stance, but Matsumura just stood in a natural posture. He seemingly had no chance to defend himself, so the engraver initiated an attack. As soon as this occurred, Matsumura opened his eyes wide, and a power seemed to stop the attacker. His gaze physically drained the opponent's energy, so much so that the engraver had to sit down. This same thing happened a couple more times, and both times the result was the same: the engraver had to quit his attack and sit down. His energy had been pulled out of him. He had no ki. This confused the engraver, who could not understand what was occurring. However, he did not want to give up, so he launched one more attack. This time, Matsumura let out a loud *kiai*, a vocal energy projection, and the engraver was halted in his tracks. The bout was over, even though a single blow had not been struck.

"Practicing irimi leads to a dominating feeling, and it eventually eliminates the idea of defense."

O-Sensei displayed similar skills, as did some of his students. John Stevens described such power in *Abundant Peace*:

> "One's kiai, a forceful inner and outer projection of kokyu and ki power, indicates the level of one's coordination of body and mind. Kiai is usually thought of as merely the shout emitted at the instant a technique is executed. For most trainees, this is true, but for advanced practitioners a kiai is a perfectly concentrated burst of energy, only part of which is audible. [O-Sensei's] kiai was, not surprisingly, irresistible. "Use your kiai as a weapon," he instructed his disciples."[41]

One story involves him attending a service at a Buddhist temple, and although O-Sensei was not Buddhist, he joined in the recitation of the *Heart Sutra*. It is said that those present felt a physical effect in their bodies from his chanting. On another occasion, he was demonstrating his new art, and a newspaper company president was in the audience. He and others in attendance believed that the feats he displayed were fake, that is, until O-Sensei let out a terrific kiai, which supposedly damaged the flashbulbs in attendants' cameras. Other stories relate that he, like Matsumura, stopped challengers with a glance alone. Certainly, sometimes historical facts are exaggerated, but such stories appear frequently in the history of many different martial arts, from countries all over the world. This indicates that this power is something real, something to be explored. And how to gain such skills is not a mystery.

Aiki and Kiai

Aiki and kiai alike are not new terms. They appear in old records of various ryu. The two are used almost interchangeably in some cases, and they are written with the same characters. Some students mistakenly think of Aiki as "harmony" or something like that, but the term means nothing similar. In Daito-ryu Aikijujutsu, it refers to a specific technique that literally renders the opponent powerless. O-Sensei sometimes expanded the term's meaning to cover some of his religious ideals as well as the martial concept adopted from Takeda's art. As a result, there are all sorts of misguided notions about what Aiki is. Originally, it was said to be like thunder and lightning, but such an obscure connection will not help anyone to understand. Aiki is balancing yin and yang, while kiai is a bit different. Both require intent. Kiai literally translates to "spirit joining". Today, some understand it as a loud scream used to disrupt or frighten your opponent, but this is not in the least bit accurate. When everything merges and functions in a coordinated manner, yin and yang are balanced and kiai and Aiki alike exist.

"When everything merges and functions in a coordinated manner, yin and yang are balanced and kiai and Aiki alike exist."

Kiai has an inherent feeling, a feeling that everything is just right. Different classifications of kiai exist: initiating, withdrawing, and completing. Initiating kiai is explosive and should match your technique. Withdrawing kiai has the feeling that you are pulling back into yourself as you break away from an encounter. Kiai at a technique's completion appears as a successful technique reaches its peak. This peak is called kime. Every technique has a flow like an ocean wave. It starts small, gathers momentum, and then peaks before breaking, and once it breaks, it subsides and melds once again with the infinite ocean from which it emerged. Kiai is associated with *zanshin*, the concept of a remaining mind. In an art like kyudo, zanshin is understood as the unreleased mind. One focuses his attention on the target, so much so that he merges with it. Everything else disappears, so only the target it left. In this way, the arrow will find its mark (because nothing but the target exists). Once the arrow is released, the mind is not. It remains. This is zanshin. It is the goal of serious practitioners of any art, including calligraphy, swordsmanship, and even the tea ceremony. Kiai encompasses this mindset, but it also includes an expansive feeling. Extend energy in all directions. In this way, you are larger than your physical form.

The Breath of Life

Outside the martial arts, your actions influence others, whether you know it or not. Everything and everyone is connected, and O-Sensei referred to the invisible connective tissues as the Breath of Life. Terms like this are only in place so people can discuss the phenomenon. Such concepts are beyond words. Enlightened individuals use words to lead practitioners in the correct direction, but they can only point the way. Each student must discover the path for himself. Once on it, a long and arduous journey awaits. If he sticks with it, he will eventually reach his goal, and all will become clear. Consider the connection between people, and think of what an expansive mentality will do. It has real power, and it connects to ideas of irimi and atemi. This atemi, whether it issues from one's eyes, kiai, or in other ways, can be used to dominate an opponent and gain the advantage.

Striking for Real

When students train in the dojo, they often do not wish to hurt their partners, so they do not use real strikes. Their strikes stop short of the target or they have no power behind them. This is a bad practice. Instead, strike for real. If the opponent does not deal with it quickly enough, he will get hurt. If he is not skillful enough to deal with it, and you see that he is going to get hit, stop the strike. But do not begin striking in an inefficient manner; do not use a fake strike. Strike for real, then stop it if you need to. This is seemingly just a change in mentality, but it is much more. It is a change in intent, and it manifests physically. Consider that you are holding a sword. When the opponent moves to cut, use the concept of isshin itto. Cut through with the intention of cutting the attacker in half. You own him. Cut through and dominate him. If he doesn't get out of the way, stop your sword, but do not strike with the intention of stopping short of the target from the onset.

Now, remove the sword and stand there empty-handed. Invite your opponent to attack. As he moves, mentally raise your sword and cut him. Do it for real. Use kiai. Cut. Your intent will be palpable, and your opponent will react to it. You can change his attack by force of will alone. The more you work on this, the more powerful your intent will become. This is mind atemi. There might not be any physical contact at all, but your spiritual dominance will stymie the opponent, making him adjust and attack in a different way. Such an atemi must be used at the onset of any technique. When an opponent attacks, use atemi to change or halt his movement. The founder said Aikido is 75-percent striking. Other shihan have said it is even more. This is how atemi *is* Aikido, whether one can see a physical strike or not. Consider this phenomenon, and then work to add it to all Aikido techniques. Strive to make it the most important aspect of your movement. Then use the kokyu training methods that O-Sensei passed down to strengthen your intent and become even more powerful.

7.4 Hold a sword and invite your opponent to attack.

7.5 Cut him for real. Your intent will halt his movement and, (hopefully), unbalance him. It will at least make him change his intended attack.

7.6 Now, remove the sword but keep the same mentality: that of cutting the attacker. Whether it is effective or not depends on the attacker's skill level.

7.7 If the attacker is susceptible to it, he will pause, his attack stymied.

7.8 Once you see this reaction, the kuzushi, enter and take control.

7.9-7.12 A possible conclusion once kuzushi occurs.

PART III. JODAN (ADVANCED) LEVEL: KOKYU POWER

Michi (The Way) — Calligraphy by Walther G. von Krenner

8

O-SENSEI'S POWER

Stories about martial artists who possess seemingly superhuman strength abound. Sometimes, the skills displayed are misunderstood, and people who do not know any better start to think that such people gained "divine powers" or "universal strength." This is a mistake. Focus on their actual feats, and know that there are ways to develop such powers. O-Sensei himself, in an interview in 1932, stated that anyone could learn to do what he could do. In the book *Shinrei no Hiyaku: Genshutsu no Chojin* (*The Spirit Leaps Forward: Emergence of the Superhuman*), author Miura Kanzou interviewed O-Sensei, who at the time went by the name Moritaka. Miura opened the interview with the following:

> "Miyamoto Musashi is long deceased, and so it may be that the secrets of that extraordinary Budo have not been received by the ordinary people of today. Accordingly, I would like to speak just a little about a modern figure who was thought by some to have surpassed Musashi, Mr. Moritaka Ueshiba. Mr. Ueshiba currently has a dojo in the Ushigome area of Tokyo. This gentleman was hidden from the public eye until two or three years ago, and that this astonishing true Budo existed in the world was unknown."[42]

Then, it goes on to explain that in the spring of Showa 5 (1930), O-Sensei engaged in contests at the Imperial Japanese Army Academy. He took on large, powerfully-built fifth- and sixth-dan Judo practitioners. When they stepped up the following occurred:

> "They were broken and played with like kittens. Even when the contest began with three strong men grasping his neck and arms, they were blown away like pieces of paper. No

Signed photograph of O-Sensei

matter their rank in kendo, whoever came was unable to touch him with their swords and they'd be struck and fall with a thud. The young representatives of the Kodokan were like children before tengu, handled without issue."[43]

The text continues to provide such background information in the introduction, and, although there is a tendency to dramatize actual occurrences in literary works, this book was not meant as such. It is non-fiction, and other accounts of pre-war Ueshiba support the claims made in this text. Nevertheless, the important points of this book, to the extent of its illumination of Aikido skills, are revealed in the interview with O-Sensei. The author cited several occasions in which O-Sensei demonstrated incredible powers, and he asked, "Is there a method for gaining power that you have used? Or is it something mystical?"

O-Sensei said, "There is a definite method."[44]

Mr. Miura then asked, "Can that method be learned by everybody?"[45]

"It can," O-Sensei replied.[46]

This relates to something Takeda Sensei once said regarding the method to gain such power: he had to be careful who he taught because Aiki was so easy to learn. There was a definite method used to teach students how to develop and then use such power. Mr. Miura asked O-Sensei how much power he actually has. His reply was the following: "Normally, the same as a normal person, but when I put some effort into it, I can carry around two bags of rice while wearing geta without a problem."[47]

He then went on to demonstrate something even more fantastic. He extended his right arm, and asked three of his students who were present to hang from it. This they did with O-Sensei showing no noticeable strain. It might sound incredible, but there are still men alive today who have this skill and who can demonstrate it to others. It is

> "Learning the principles behind the techniques and the actual technique of Aiki is more important than individual pins and throws."

O-Sensei's Power

not a magic trick. There is a definite method to learning and improving this skill. While conducting the interview, Mr. Miura was obviously shocked to see O-Sensei holding up three students with seemingly no effort. O-Sensei explained it to him:

> "However strong the opponent is, when I stand to face them the power to overcome them, power that I don't myself understand, comes forth. Moreover, I don't know anything about what kind of an art Shinto-ryu is, but when I contest with Shinto-ryu's Mr. Otsuka, my hands become completely Shinto-ryu hands. When I meet with a Judo-ka, my hands become the hands of Judo. I become completely transparent, the opponent is transformed into their best real body and I am possessed by my guardian spirit. The other person disappears and I am just attacked by their hands and form. The more that the other person's shugyo has progressed, the greater their real body and their guardian spirit, so I must also become greater. In any case, the state of my heart when facing an opponent is as transparent as a mirror, so in this state the other person's spirit is perfectly revealed."[48]

It is difficult to follow O-Sensei's lectures primarily because he was an ardent Omoto-kyo follower: a religion that some believed was a divisive cult. However, O-Sensei had power, as did many other students of Takeda Sensei. One of the most skilled students to have studied with him was Sagawa Yukiyoshi, who constantly talked about internal power using the same term that O-Sensei used (in the interview) above: transparent power. He wrote, "Through the process of tempering my body, I realized that in abandoning my quest for power, my true strength emerged. I temporarily named this power the 'Transparent Power.'"[49]

> "You begin to see things in a new, expansive way, and you can neutralize any attack."

He met Takeda Sensei when he was ten years old. Horikawa Taiso met Takeda on a train and they spoke about martial arts. Takeda Sensei gave him some kind of a demonstration, which impressed Horikawa so much that he invited the man to Yubetsu, Hokkaido to teach. When Takeda showed up, Horikawa gathered the neighbors and anyone else in town who shared interest in the martial arts. Among those in attendance was Sagawa Sensei's father Nenokichi. Apparently, his performance was legendary. His arms bound behind him, Takeda Sensei asked everyone present to attack. He easily controlled or threw them all. When others tried to grab his legs and hoist him from the ground, they were forced into it. He was immovable, seemingly attached to the ground. Obviously impressed with both his techniques and his unusual power, many of those present began studying with him. Sagawa's father had a special request; he told Takeda that since he was old, he would prefer to learn Aiki instead of techniques.

This indicates that Aiki is separate from techniques. It can be applied within techniques, but techniques are unnecessary to manifest Aiki. This is further supported by statements made by both O-Sensei and Takeda Sensei. Ueshiba knew Sagawa Nenokichi well because he often went to his shop to buy rice and miso paste. Eventually, the elder Sagawa taught O-Sensei some Daito-ryu, which he had learned from Takeda, and O-Sensei was so impressed he wanted to meet Takeda Sensei himself. One of Nenokichi's fellow students, Kotaru Yoshida set up the meeting at the Hisata Inn in Engaru, Hokkaido, and the rest is history. Ueshiba Sensei became obsessed with Daito-ryu Aikijujutsu, and eventually taught the art. Takeda gave him a *kyoju dairi* certificate in 1916. In *Morihei Ueshiba, the Founder of Aikido*, Ueshiba Kisshomaru wrote:

> "Over the course of practicing morning to night every day for one month, the Founder was very shocked by *Daito-ryu* secret techniques. Although the founder had strong power, he was outmatched."[50]

Sagawa Sensei watched the men train with Takeda Sensei from the time he was ten years old, and then eventually trained with him for years. He stated that Takeda Sensei often taught sword techniques, and "he was a genius with the sword. His swordsmanship was on a totally different dimension. Had he lived in the latter days of the Tokugawa Shogunate, he would undoubtedly have been famous."[51] Although Sagawa spent time with Takeda and learned informally from him, he did not become enrolled as a formal student until age seventeen. His father warned him that he must concentrate on learning Aiki rather than the skillful techniques (of Daito-ryu), because if he did not understand the true essence of Takeda's instruction, his time would be wasted. Thus, learning the principles behind the techniques and the actual technique of Aiki is more important than individual pins and throws. Decades after beginning his training with Takeda Sensei, Sagawa Sensei wrote:

> "By taking the stance that Aiki is a technique, that something is there, you can slowly begin to understand it. Nothing will come out of the thinking that Aiki is the flow or ki or the art of go no sen. When you come to understand Aiki, as soon as someone mentions "the flow of ki," you'll know that he knows nothing."[52]

Sagawa explained that once you can manifest Aiki, an entirely different mindset emerges. You begin to see things in a new, expansive way, and you can neutralize any attack. Aiki can also manifest in strikes, and Sagawa used to practice his striking techniques for hours, like O-Sensei did. One of his students, Tastsuo Kimura said, "Once Sagawa told me, "Avoid my punch!" and I tried to avoid his right punch with my right hand. But his was almost three times faster than mine, and I could not avoid him at all. I felt as if he knew what I would do before I did it. It was a very strange feeling."[53]

Sagawa Sensei traveled with Takeda Sensei as his assistant, and they taught people in Fukushima, Sendai, and other prefectures. Many seminars were held for police officers or other government officials. At some of them, the participants were too afraid of Takeda Sensei, so Sagawa Sensei had to demonstrate techniques instead. At other seminars, Sagawa was uke for Takeda. This continued until Sagawa Sensei was about 35 years old, when he traveled around teaching the art as his instructor had. He commented on his skills at the time:

> "Back then, I didn't have the ability to knock someone down with only a slight movement of my body. When I was traveling all over the place teaching, I was so busy that I did not have enough time for contemplation as I do now. After settling down in my current house, I've been coming to many new realizations. You can't very well do that

without giving yourself the time and the space for it. No matter how much you train and temper your body, you can't improve unless you keep working on your techniques and figuring out how they might be applied and under what circumstances. Simply continuing your practice for training without giving any thought to what you're doing doesn't lead to true progress.[54]

"By looking at his teachings, we can discover the way to attain immovability and the ability to demonstrate an unstoppable force."

Among the important things that Sagawa Yukiyoshi has passed down, things he learned from Takeda Sokaku, are the following:

1. Aiki is a technique. It is not something mystical. This was also explained by O-Sensei, who said in an interview that there was a definite method to learning this kind of power, and anyone can learn it. He further explained that "Aiki cannot be understood by observing the external. You render your opponent powerless through an internal action that is not visible on the outside."[55]

2. To display Aiki and demonstrate the unstoppable force that Takeda, Ueshiba, Sagawa and others have demonstrated, it is necessary to completely relax, and to never tighten up your muscles when performing a technique. Sagawa said, "What's important is learning to relax your shoulders and to build a body that doesn't tense up."[56]

O-Sensei's student Tohei Koichi also talked about the importance of remaining relaxed and never tightening up. In fact, he said it was the most valuable thing that O-Sensei taught him. Tohei Sensei, like Takeda, Ueshiba, Sagawa and others, displayed immovability, and there are photographs and videos of his students unsuccessfully trying to push him or lift him from the ground. Anyone who has internal power possesses this skill. They cannot pretend to have it; they can prove it. Such skills are found in all countries. The Taijiquan teacher Yang Ch'eng Fu was once walking when a pedicab hit him from behind. Yang did not budge, but the cab rebounded ten feet and overturned, emptying its passengers into the street.[57] An Internet search of Chen Yu or Chen Xiaowang will produce a variety of videos in which many people are trying to unbalance these immovable instructors. This skill has been passed down to modern generations of Budo practitioners.

O-Sensei developed such skills through the practice of solo drills. Certain practices originated in China, such as funakogi undo, which is a Southern Shaolin practice. Other techniques likewise have origins in China. This is because there is a definite method to developing internal skills. O-Sensei often quoted the Taiji classics when teaching about Aiki, and his skills match those seen in China. Takeda possibly learned Aiki and internal power from Saigo Tanomo, who might not have been Japanese. Also known as Chikanori Hoshina, his family members were likely descendants of Chinese people who served the Tokugawa Shogunate as instructors of Chinese arts and sciences, and also taught martial arts.[58] The Hoshina family had their own martial art, which included sword forms using a Chinese-style blade, which was shorter and thicker than Japanese blades.[59] In addition, in some Daito-ryu texts, the name Chikanori Hoshina is either replaced by or appended with the term *chugokujin* (Chinese person). Clearly, these techniques were introduced to the Aizu domain through China. Whether the techniques of internal power cultivation began in Tibet, India or other countries is a matter of debate outside this text's purview, but it is clear that there is a definitive method for attaining such skills. Tohei Sensei spent years obsessed with their attainment, and he laid down the important points for his students. By looking at his teachings, we can discover the way to attain immovability and the ability to demonstrate an unstoppable force.

9

TOHEI SENSEI'S BACKGROUND

Tohei likely first began learning how to develop internal power at a dojo called the Ichikukai, where practitioners trained in demanding austerities conveyed by Tesshu Yamaoka, one of the greatest martial artists in Japanese history. (As an interesting side note, in various circumstances, Tesshu demonstrated solidity; when challengers tried to shove him around, he was rooted to the ground like a tree.[60]) When Tohei Sensei first arrived at the dojo, he was young and sickly, and the senior students wouldn't allow him through the door. They explained how difficult the training was and they doubted that he could withstand it. Tohei Sensei did not back down. He was determined to grow stronger or die trying. The chief instructor Hino Tesso was impressed and decided to give him a chance. They allowed him to sit in meditation (zazen), but they would not let him engage in more difficult ascetic practices until he had strengthened his body through such seated exercise.

Tohei Sensei, talking about this period of his life, said that he would spend the entire night in seated meditation.[61] After about six months, his teacher recognize that he was strong enough to begin harsher training. It was at this point that he began misogi practices, which made him physically strong.[62] When he engaged in Judo matches, he was able to throw everyone without difficulty. He thought about quitting martial arts because the other practitioners no longer posed a challenge. It was then that Mori Shohei, one of his seniors, told him about Ueshiba Morihei.

He showed up at Ueshiba's dojo and was first greeted by a student named Matsumoto. Tohei asked what Aikido was, and the student asked him to grasp his wrist. Tohei understood that he was about to demonstrate a technique and reached out with his left hand. Matsumoto applied nikkyo, and although it was painful, Tohei was unimpressed; in fact, he considered leaving right then. At that moment, O-Sensei appeared and offered a demonstration. He threw one of the larger live-in students around the dojo as though he were a ragdoll, and like other observers at different times and in different places, Tohei Sensei thought it was all fake. O-Sensei invited him to attack as well, and he did. Tohei Sensei later explained, "I got into a Judo stance and moved in to grab him. To my great surprise, he threw me so smoothly and swiftly that I couldn't even figure out what had happened."[63] He joined the dojo immediately and trained daily. He was amazed at O-Sensei's power, and he couldn't understand how some of the techniques were performed. He said:

> "I found the training very strange and mysterious, and I was dying to know how the techniques were done. When someone uses power to throw you, there's always something you can do to react or counter. But it's a different story when the person isn't doing anything in particular and you're still getting thrown. [...] In the beginning, I had no idea what was going on."[64]

According to Tohei Sensei, when he first began training with O-Sensei, he was the weakest person in the dojo despite having been the strongest in his Judo club; even high school students practicing with Ueshiba could throw him. Nevertheless, he trained daily in Aikido and continued to practice both zazen and misogi at the Ichikukai. The esoteric training to which he devoted himself was exhausting, and often, after training the entire night, he went directly to the dojo to train in Aikido. He found that the other students were unable to throw him after such training. He was exhausted, and he had released his muscular power. This was Tohei Sensei's first realization of the relaxation's power. He watched O-Sensei more closely and realized that he never put power into techniques. He was always completely relaxed, and this relaxation, when performed correctly, was a source of unlimited and unstoppable power. (He might have also learned esoteric practices to develop power from Nakamura Tempu, with whom he trained. Nakamura founded Shin Shin Toitsu Do, an art which incorporates many Indian yoga techniques.)

Tohei Sensei was influential in bringing Aikido to the West, and when he arrived, some martial artists, who as a whole were much larger than he was, challenged him. He quickly learned that Aikido techniques performed in a sharp and powerful manner were not effective.[65] But, when he relaxed completely and then used the techniques, real power manifested. It was then that he realized that what O-Sensei said and what he did were different. He explained:

> "For example, despite the fact that he himself was very relaxed, he told his students to do sharp, powerful techniques. When I got to Hawaii, there were guys as strong as Akebono and Konishiki (two well-known Hawaiian sumo wrestlers) all over the place. There is just no way to use force or power to prevail against that kind of strength. When you're firmly pinned or controlled, the parts of your body that are pinned directly simply can't move. All you can do was start a movement from those parts that you can move, and the only way to do that successfully is to relax. Even if your opponent has you with all his strength, you can still send him flying if you relaxed when you do your throw."[66]

It is interesting that certain expressions show up in the teachings of people who have real internal power and Aiki. Sagawa Yukiyoshi explains the importance of learning how to relax, and figuring out what your body could do when it was completely pinned. He determined that even when completely pinned to the ground, there was always something that could be moved, something that could allow you a way out of a technique. Such skills could not be developed without relaxation. However, the term relaxation will be misunderstood by the majority of people who read it. It is also possible that there was nothing more than a linguistic confusion when Tohei Sensei said that O-Sensei did and said different things. Perhaps the terms used were understood in different ways by these two men. When Tohei heard "use sharp, powerful techniques," he perhaps thought that O-Sensei was referring to muscular strength, while O-Sensei himself might have recognized the true power that emerged from

"O-Sensei and Tohei Sensei had a type of internal power or transparent power which they both developed through esoteric training."

Tohei Sensei demonstrates a power-building exercise: funa-kogi undo (c. 1968). Behind him are Walther von Krenner and Robert Frager.

his feeling of relaxation. Such terms might always be a source of debate, but it is clear that both O-Sensei and Tohei Sensei had a type of internal power or transparent power which they both developed through esoteric training. Tohei Sensei trained at the Ichikukai, while O-Sensei trained with Takeda and at the Omoto-kyo compound. Takeda Sensei also had such power, as did Sagawa Sensei and many other Daito-ryu Aikijujutsu and Aikido students.

O-Sensei tried to convey such principles to his students, but because of his obsession with religious teachings, he always used spiritual terms, quoting obscure passages from the *Kojiki*, *Nihon Shoki*, or Omoto sacred texts. When Tohei Sensei was asked when O-Sensei learned how to relax, he replied that he thought O-Sensei learned it while training at the Omoto-kyo compound in Ayabe. O-Sensei had described a sensation that overcame him while he was standing near a well and wiping his face after a hard training. He felt like he was surrounded by light and understood that he had an indestructible body. It was then that he felt he was "one with the Universe." However, if the religious terms and connotation were swept away, he is describing what others have experienced: the realization of a true power source within.

This idea of relaxation must be understood because many people who hear it, if they do not understand what Tohei Sensei and other like him were referring to, would let their anatomical system break down. They might slouch, their spines bent, leaning in such a way that their entire skeletal structures become nothing more than bags of bones. This is not what great martial artists refer to as relaxation. Luckily, Tohei Sensei explicitly explained how to develop such power. Certainly, if you engaged in correct zazen or properly performed misogi exercises, you could likely develop such skills faster and in a more comprehensive manner, but Tohei Sensei left instructions that everyone can follow. Everyone can be successful using his method. Then, once you understand the basics, you can explore such methods and the power that they develop more fully on your own. He did not give instructions for individuals who already had internal power; he rather left a trail for initiates to follow. Once you set upon this path, do not give up. Continue, and you can one day attain the skills of the great teachers.

10

TOHEI'S FOUR BASIC PRINCIPLES

Although it is not suggested that students actually try this exercise, Tohei Sensei mentioned what he called "the floating bridge" in one of his books. A person lies down on the ground. Another grabs his ankles. A third person grabs his training uniform in the area near his shoulders, and while supporting his head, the two standing individuals lift the prone person. The aim is to keep the spine straight, and the body in the same relative position as it is lifted off the ground. If the person being lifted tenses his body, he will break in the center. In other words, the spine will not remain straight, and the center of the body will droop toward the floor. If the person on the ground relaxes, the result will be the same. The body will droop. One thing can change this. If the person being lifted relaxes completely and considers that "a steel rod runs from the top of his head to the tips of his toes" his body will maintain its original shape.[67] It will not droop.

Another previously mentioned exercise is the so-called unbendable arm. If the doer completely relaxes his arm and considers energy emanating from his fingers, the arm will not bend. Combine these two teachings. Instead of thinking of the spine as a stationary steel rod, feel that the rod is moving up and down. The energy of the spine should move upward and downward. In Chinese (internal) arts, practitioners are often taught to feel as though their heads were suspended from above. Feel like you are stretching the spine upward while relaxing as much as you can. This will make you stronger, and it is a starting point for Tohei Sensei's four principles for unifying the mind and body:

1. Keep one point.
2. Relax completely.
3. Keep weight underside.
4. Extend Ki.

Keeping one point means concentrating the energy into the hara, which in ancient times was considered the soul's residence in Japan. It is impossible to say exactly where this is within the abdomen, because the hara is not a specific place defined by organs, muscles, or fascia. It is the energy center of the body, and after fixing your mind on this point while training, it takes over. Every martial artist should strive to move from center, so all the body's movements actually initiate from hara. In this sense, energy starts in this location and then expands outward. This is what Tohei Sensei called extending ki.

> "Keeping one point means concentrating the energy into the hara, which in ancient times was considered the soul's residence in Japan."

It is easy to find out if you are doing this correctly or not. Kneel on the ground (in seiza) and have your partner push you. Start with a gentle push to the chest and then have him gradually increase the pressure. As he does so, consider that the spine is being pulled up and down, that it is a steadily expanding steel rod. Ask him for feedback. He should feel a noticeable change within you. Maintaining this feeling, concentrate on the center of the hara, and then extend ki in all directions. You will find that he cannot unbalance you, and that you have become much stronger, even though it might seem to you that you are weaker. This is because it is an unusual feeling, perhaps the first time you have ever experienced your true strength. O-Sensei made many comments about true strength versus physical strength, and said that he only became strong after he ceased trying to be strong. In other words, do not try to be strong. Do not use your muscles. This is what Tohei Sensei referred to as relaxing completely.

For some people, this is easier said than done, because the natural reaction of most people when they are attacked is to tighten up. They flex their muscles when being pinned or trying to pin someone, and they have a fall sense that such an action makes them stronger. Tohei Sensei wrote, "This notion arises from the illusion that when one is relaxed he is weak. The fact is that if you relax properly you are very strong."[68] Only while relaxing completely can you maintain the one point and extend energy in all directions. In addition, if you tense your muscles your center of gravity tends to rise, making you easier to throw. You can test this. Flex all your muscles while standing and ask your partner to throw you with a hip throw or a shoulder throw. Then, consider the expanding energy of the spine, concentrate on the point in the hara, and extend energy in all directions while completely relaxing. Now, ask him to throw you again, and you will find that you are rooted, making it more difficult, if not impossible, to upset your balance. Once you have tried this, reverse roles. Have your partner flex and you try to throw him, and then have him relax completely and do the same. There will be no doubt that relaxation has a certain type of strength within it, and this strength is without doubt superior to muscular strength.

The third principle is to keep weight underside, and in addition to the other thoughts (the spinal extension, keeping one point, relaxing completely, and extending ki), this is important to keep in mind. Tohei Sensei explained:

> "The weight of every object naturally settles at its lowest point. Since the body of a man is also an object, if he relaxes completely, the weight of every part should naturally be settled at the lowest point. Living calmness is a state where the weight of an object naturally settles underside. So, if a man relaxes completely he can always remain calm. This is third of the Four Basic Principles. If we keep one point, we can relax. If we relax, the weight of every part of our body is at the lowest point. The first, second, and the third of the Four Basic Principles are inseparable."[69]

You can test this principle as well. Here is an easy way to do it: thrust your arm out in front of you and ask your training partner to push up on the arm. He will move you easily. Then, while keeping one point, thrust your arm out in front of you again, but this time relax completely, and consider that energy is flowing out your fingertips. Have him move your arm again. He will find it more difficult. Finally, keep weight underside by thinking of the lower edge of the arm. Feel more energy on the arm's underside. This will make the arm even more difficult to raise. Reverse roles and try it again, and you will see just how heavy and seemingly immovable this practice makes your entire body.

O-Sensei used to have his students push him. Videos and photographs show many of them pushing on his chest, head, or arm. It is clear that he was working on this. O-Sensei also spent time practicing alone. He did exercises like funa-kogi undo repeatedly. In a modern Aikido dojo, practitioners do not seem to spend much time daily doing solo exercises. They also rarely do push tests, in which practitioners push on each other to work on their relaxation while extending energy and keeping their weight underside. If students truly want to become as good as O-Sensei was, they should do what he did. They should practice the things he practiced.

11

O-SENSEI'S SOLO TRAINING DRILLS

One of the exercises that O-Sensei did constantly (according to his students) was the so-called funa-kogi undo, or boat rowing exercise. Stand with your feet shoulder-width apart, and then step forward with your left foot. Your right knee will bend and your left will straighten as you use your spine to pull your hands and arms back to your torso. Then, your right knee straightens, your left bends, and your spine moves in the opposite direction as you thrust your hands out in front of you. In motion, this looks like the same movement used to row a boat, hence the exercise's name. While you are performing it, you want to maintain the one point while extending energy in all directions.

You also want to relax completely and keep weight underside. At all positions in this drill, you should be stable and immovable. Have a training partner check this. Have him push on your arms, shoulders, knees, head, back, etc. You should be stable, and he should not be able to move you. According to Tohei Sensei, if you properly maintain the one point, your partner will be unable to budge you. If, however, you lose that point, your partner will be able to break your balance easily. Here are some suggestions: if you are having difficulty remaining rooted to the ground, and you are losing the one point, make sure you are not shifting your weight during the exercise. Even though your knees are bending and unbending, you should always remain centered. Viewed from the side, if you drew an imaginary line through the center of the practitioner's head all the way to the ground, his head and center should not move off that line as he performs funa-kogi undo. Never shift your weight front or back, because if your weight is on one side you can be easily thrown. To avoid this, practice remaining centered throughout the movement.

It is easy to trick yourself into thinking that you already do this. The only way to check for sure is to have your training partner attempt to push you over.

O-Sensei demonstrates funa-kogi undo.
Credit: From the collection of Walther von Krenner

First, do it while standing still and working on Tohei Sensei's four principles. Then, test it in motion. Walk across the dojo floor and have your training partner push you whenever he thinks there is a weakness. Various training methods are used in both Chinese and Japanese martial arts to help students maintain the one-point in motion. It is possible that O-Sensei chose funa-kogi undo, ikkyo undo, and other similar exercises because such practices were efficacious for him in attaining this skill. If you want to gain the same skills that he displayed, devote some serious time practicing the same exercises.

Another is ikkyo undo. Like the previous exercise, strive to keep the one point throughout. Again, take a small step forward with your left foot. Both arms should be relaxed and by your sides, but make sure the arms are not dead. Enliven them with energy. Extend your fingers and then move the arms up to eye-level, making sure that you do not raise your shoulders. Keep them down where they belong. A common error is to raise the shoulders anytime the arms are moved forward. You need to spend a ton of time working to stop this common, incorrect movement. Even when throwing punches or performing arm or wristlocks, make sure the shoulders do not rise. If they do, you will lose all your power. Solo-training exercises like ikkyo undo teach practitioners how to use the shoulders and arms correctly, but understanding will not suddenly appear. You should work on this and other drills daily, for years.

After raising your arms in front of you, pause and correct anything that might be incorrect. Make sure that your weight has not shifted, even though your left knee bent and your right knee straightened as your hands rose.

O-Sensei demonstrates ikkyo-undo.
Credit: From the collection of Walther von Krenner

Also, make sure that you are extending energy in all directions. In time, this will develop a more connected body, and it will provide more power in all of your techniques and strikes. Once the arms are up, it is time to bring them back down. Feel as though you are striking something with your shuto. This feeling will force you to keep weight underside. In other words, while thinking about striking, the energy is on the underside of the arm. As the arms are returning, the left knee straightens and the right knee bends. Continue practicing this for a bit, and then switch the position of your legs and work on the other side. Tohei Sensei pointed out some important points in his book *Ki in Daily Life*:

> "[In ikkyo undo], B should perform tests of A's stability as he goes through this exercise. A must constantly maintain the one point and hold his upper body straight. Though at a glance it might seem that the exercise would be more powerful if we tensed our arms, the reverse is true. If we tense up, our opponent can easily move us around anywhere he likes. Keep the weight of the upper body always in the one point, and keep the body's central line straight. Working from this line and using the shoulder joint as the center and the length of the arm as the radius, move your arms to describe a semicircle with your fingertips. If you shorten or extend the length of the radius during the process, you will not make a circle. Since ki is always flowing out from your fingertips, extend your arms to the fullest and you will generate great centrifugal power."[70]

After doing this on both sides, you can turn. Raise your arms to the front when your right foot is forward, bring the arms down, and then pivot on your feet to face the opposite direction. Make sure that you do not rise as you turn. Keep your head and hips level. Facing the opposite direction, now with your left foot forward, complete the same exercise. Then repeat it. Ikkyo undo, like funa-kogi undo, should be practiced daily, and you should spend a great deal of time mastering the four points of mind-body coordination that Tohei Sensei taught.

O-Sensei taught the same things, but his vernacular was different. For example, he said, "Circles are vacant. To be vacant is to be free and unrestricted. When a center arises in vacancy, it brings forth ki. Spirit lies in the center of vacancy when this is in accord with the infinite universe. Spirit is the source of whole creation, mother of eternity. It is a circle with spirit in it that helps man prosper in oneness of his body and mind."[71] These are examples of the types of statements that he made. Tohei Sensei similarly talked about how keeping the one point can help you to unify mind and body and then merge with the universe. It is possible that some of O-Sensei's language just rubbed off on him, but it is more likely that Tohei Sensei was religious and spiritual in his own way, based upon his training period at the Ichikukai dojo among other places.

The power that emanates from one's center after he or she learns how to relax completely and extend energy from center has been called a Divine energy by many practitioners in diverse traditions. This might be because the less you do physically the stronger you become. As soon as you remove your own force, in other words, as soon as you stop trying to do something to an opponent, you become centered, keeping the one point, and real power flows. Daily training in such internal exercises will make you more powerful. You will slowly decrease the amount of muscular force used, and increase full-body power, which flows from the center. This training will benefit all your techniques, and it will make you extremely difficult to throw or even move. In time, it will seem like you are rooted to the ground. You will gain the same skill that Tohei Koichi and Ueshiba Morihei O-Sensei displayed. Instead of putting such incredible practitioners on pedestals, looking up to them and admiring what they have done, strive to equal them. If you believe you cannot ever do what they have done, you create a self-fulfilling prophecy. It is far better to admire their accomplishments, and then strive to equal or even surpass them.

"The true source of power in Aikido is not within the varied techniques, but rather in the internal training exercises that have been overlooked by many practitioners."

We know both Tohei Sensei and O-Sensei practiced alone every day. They never stopped. Perhaps this tells us that the true source of power in Aikido is not within the varied techniques, but rather in the internal training exercises

O-Sensei merged the martial and spiritual paths, so he used religious terms to describe martial power that anyone can attain through the correct performance of certain exercises.
Credit: From the collection of Walther von Krenner

that have been overlooked by many practitioners. Some consider them just a part of dojo warm-ups, akin to stretching exercises. Rethink them in their entirety. Try to do them while keeping Tohei's four basic principles, and do them all the time. The power that you will eventually be able to generate can be applied to striking, pinning, and throwing. It will make you an overall proficient practitioner.

CONCLUSION

Striking is complex. While outsiders might view it as a simple topic, there are sophisticated ways to use the body for striking purposes. Whether practitioners use fists, hand blades, fingers, elbows, knees, head, or other body parts, deciding what to use and when to use it is integrally linked to where they are striking. Hard and soft areas must be considered, and the most effective strike must be chosen based upon the intended target. Some strikes can disable the opponent, and practitioners of any art should be aware of such possibilities. They should train to strike correctly and develop power, so if the need to end an engagement quickly and decisively arises, they are capable of doing so. O-Sensei said that Budo's original intent was to kill an adversary with a single blow.

He also spoke about how powerful Aikido's strikes are. And although this might seem anachronistic to some modern practitioners, he had such power, and he taught his students to use it. If you are going to study an art like Aikido, isn't it better to do what the founder did? To study what he taught? If so, make sure your Aikido is martially effective. Make sure you can handle yourself in a variety of both orthodox and unorthodox situations, and strive to develop powerful atemi. In his writing, Shioda Gozo mentioned the powerful strikes that practitioners developed through Aikido, and he demonstrated such power constantly. The same is true regarding many other students who trained directly with the founder. However, such power seems to be lacking in modern practitioners. Also absent in some dojo is explicit training in how to strike, and some practitioners do not practice striking effectively. Serious students should think about this.

The entire idea of atemi in Aikido should be reconsidered. In some dojo, strikes are disregarded, and when people attack, they use incorrect, ineffective strikes. If you were actually hit with a tsuki, yokomen or shomen attack, there would be no damage. Make it a real attack, with real intent behind it. If you always strike with the intention of stopping it before it contacts uke, you will develop a bad habit. There have been cases in which people who have studied the martial arts for years ended up in real engagements and had faulty maai. They were defeated because their strikes failed to reach the target or because they overextended while striking. This overextension occurs if you try to stop your strikes short of your training partner in the dojo. You get used to being a certain distance away from the person you are striking, and you are not close enough to actually strike him. In a real situation, when you react, your body will be too far away to strike with full force, so the tendency is to overextend. Hit something real, like a heavy bag, wall-mounted pad, or freestanding dummy. Note how close you need to be. Then, take this newfound understanding of maai out for a spin when practicing waza. Work on establishing and maintaining correct maai, from where you can issue powerful blows.

> "Work on establishing and maintaining correct maai, from where you can issue powerful blows."

However, the real purpose of atemi in Aikido is not to maim or kill an opponent, as it is in some other arts. Striking in Aikido can distract an opponent. When someone shoots in to grab or strike you, a properly placed atemi can cause the attacker to stop or redirect the attack. Such a redirection is conforming to you, and if the opponent conforms to you, you can control him. O-Sensei said, "In Aikido, before one's opponent comes, one absorbs the intentions of his mind into oneself to control it freely." Once the attacker reacts to your atemi, you can apply a technique. In this way, striking opens the door to many technical possibilities. A properly placed strike also takes uke's balance, making it impossible for him to continue attacking while making it easier to throw or pin him.

Striking can similarly fix errors throughout a technique. If you apply ikkyo and uke regains his balance because your technique was imperfect, a kick or punch to the ribcage, face or lower leg might be enough to allow you to regain control and complete the pin. This can work from the other side too: when you are being pinned. Find opportunities to strike while nage is trying to pin or throw you. Use atemi to deflect his movements and then apply a counter technique. When you sense a weakness in nage's technique, it might be difficult to simply change your position and reverse that technique or apply a counter technique, but a strike will provide time and possibilities. Do not think about applying any technique, because you do not know what your opponent will do. Instead, just think about striking, hard. Once this occurs, techniques will become available. O-Sensei said that Aikido is 75-percent strikes. This is why.

Using Tohei's four points to unify the mind and body in conjunction with solo training drills such as ikkyo undo and funa-kogi undo will help to make your body more connected, which in turn makes your strikes stronger. Such practices will also help to increase your intent. After training for enough decades, you will eventually strengthen your intent to such a degree that you can affect those who have less skill without physical contact. Mentally cut through the opponent's attack as though it were not even there. With no fear, enter into the attack. An instructional verse in the sword art Kashima Shinryu reads, "Beneath the confronted sword is hell. Step in! There is also paradise."[72] Control the opponent. This is the principle of irimi, but if your intent is strong enough, and if your attacker is not as skilled as you are, your body posture, movements, and even your eyes can affect him.

O-Sensei had a piercing stare, and he indicated that it was possible to stop an opponent with a single glance. His teacher Takeda Sokaku also was known for his piercing gaze, as were many other accomplished martial artists. One famous incident was briefly recounted earlier in this text. It involved Matsumura and the engraver who faced off in the graveyard of Kimbu Palace, but the fight never occurred. Every time the engraver tried to attack, he felt repelled by a force that he swore emanated from Matsumura's eyes. Perhaps this is one of the highest levels of atemi. It would take years of study to even begin to develop this skill, increasing your intent to such a level that the opponent can be forestalled with a glance or slight movement alone.

When considering such possibilities and looking at the accomplishments of masters like O-Sensei, it must seem that their skills are unobtainable. However, the masters were men. Yamamoto Tsunetomo (1659-1719)

O-Sensei's piercing stare.
Credit: From the collection of Walther von Krenner

explained that it is spiritless to think you cannot attain what masters have attained. He wrote:

> "If you think you will be inferior in doing something, you will be on that road very soon. Master Ittei said, "Confucius was a sage because he had the will to become a scholar when he was fifteen years old. He was not a sage because he studied later on." This is the same as the Buddhist maxim, "First intention, then enlightenment.""[73]

Consider Aikido or any martial art that you study. Train to understand the art's physical techniques. Then, practice them repeatedly to gain proficiency. Once you have developed some skill, even if you begin teaching the art, always maintain the attitude of a student. Always know that there is much more to learn, much more to discover. This mentality, called *shoshin* in Japanese, is the only thing needed to prevent stagnation. As long as you keep a student's attitude, always looking to learn, insights will consistently appear. After learning physical techniques, a spiritual dimension will materialize, but you cannot skip steps. Do not rush to experience the art's mysticism before mastering its physical aspects, because it would be an impossible task. Instead, take time to train and study, incessantly considering the techniques and the founder's words. Also, learn from others who have studied for years. Take all that is good as your own and disregard the rest. In time, you will come to understand the art's profound principles, and this understanding will naturally lead you to the spiritual dimensions.

NOTES

1 Shioda, *Aikido: My Spiritual Journey*, 27

2 Ibid., 26

3 Pranin, *Ongaeshi: Repaying a Kindness*

4 Pranin, *Aikido Pioneers: Pre-War Era*, 284

5 Amdur, *Hidden in Plain Sight*, 134

6 Kano, *Mind over Muscle*, 85

7 Ueshiba, *A Life in Aikido*

8 We covered grappling and submission techniques in detail in the book *Aikido Ground Fighting*, available through North Atlantic Books.

9 A widespread misconception regarding sword use on Japanese battlefields holds that the sword was the samurai's primary weapon. This is untrue. In battlefield combat, the sword was considered a supplementary weapon. As Karl Friday wrote: "The sword played a [...] minor role in medieval warfare. Swords never became a key battlefield armament in Japan. They were, rather, supplementary weapons, analogous to the sidearms worn by modern soldiers" (p. 251). Analysis of battlefield wounds from the fourteenth century indicates that most wounds were caused by arrows or other projectile weapons. Few injuries were caused by swords. Suzuki Masaya analyzed documents, which recorded battlefield wounds from 1563 to 1600. Out of 584 deaths, 263 died from gunshot wounds, 126 were killed by arrows, 99 by spears, 40 had sword wounds, 30 were killed by rocks, and 26 indicated a combination of the previously mentioned weapons.

10 Ueshiba, *Budo*, 71

11 Tomiki, *Judo, Appendix: Aikido*, 31

12 Ibid., 31-32

13 Samurai were always trained to use swords as right-handers. They wore the swords on the left and drew them with the right hand. By securing the right hand, warriors could not draw the sword in a standard way.

14 See Friday "*Off the Warpath*," in *Budo Perspectives*, edited by Alexander Bennett.

15 http://www.Aikidofaq.com/interviews/daito_ryu.html

16 Although not an expert in Daito-ryu at all, co-writer Ken Jeremiah trained at Kondo Sensei's dojo for several months in 1999. This information is from his recollections.

17 Oya, "Central Issues in the Instruction of Kendo," 211

18 Ibid.

19 Ibid.

20 Ibid.

21 Kano, *Mind over Muscle*, 39-40.

22 Wilson, *Lone Samurai*, 163.

23 Ibid.

24 Ueshiba, *The Spirit of Aikido*, 89

25 Ibid.

26 Ueshiba, *Budo*, 38

27 It should be pointed out again that the authors are not experts in Daito-ryu Aikijujutsu. Their insights are from watching demonstrations and practicing the art with reputable and knowledgeable instructors.

28 O-Sensei seemingly preferred the devoiced pronunciation *kototama*, but the correct Japanese term is *kotodama*.

29 The full text was accessed here: http://www.uvm.edu/~asnider/IDAS_2011_CD/Teachers/Steve%20Llano's%20Materials/Strategy%20Books/Book%20of%20Five%20Rings%20-%20Musashi.pdf

30 This article was accessed at http://www.yamakawadojo.com/principles%20from%20ono%20ha%20itto%20ryu.pdf

31 The Japanese term *kokoro gamae* literally translates to spirit or heart stance, and as such it is problematic for translators. The idea is that one's mental stance has a direct influence on physical posture. In other words, as practitioners progress in the martial arts, they become increasingly more confident and eventually, when they stand in front of an adversary, they do not see a threat. Thus, the enemy has become no enemy. The practitioner simply stands where he is and recognizes that he is unassailable. This sounds strange, but the sentiment has been echoed by many martial artists historically. If one works on his own body and mind, he comes to understand them. Once you comprehend yourself, you can understand others. In time, this results in an unusual outlook that affects everything, including martial abilities. This mentality is called kokoro gamae in some arts. O-Sensei wrote about the connection between one's mindset and his or her bodily posture: "A good stance and posture reflect a proper state of mind."

32 http://blog.Aikidojournal.com/2011/11/29/irimi-by-ellis-amdur/

33 Ueshiba, *Budo*, 31

34 Ibid., 32

35 Ueshiba, *Art of Peace*

36 Ibid.

37 Ueshiba, *Budo*, 42

38 Ibid., 43

39 Olsen, *Tai Ji Jin*, 67

40 Ueshiba, *A Life in Aikido*, 19-20

41 Stevens, *Abundant Peace*, 72.

42 Li, *A Leap of the Spirit: Moritaka (Morihei) Ueshiba in 1932*

43 Ibid.

44 Ibid.

45 Ibid.

46 Ibid.

47 Ibid.

48 Ibid.

49 Kimura, *Transparent Power*, 75

50 Ueshiba, *Morihei Ueshiba, the Founder of Aikido*, 96

51 Kimura, *Transparent Power*, 47

52 Ibid., 150. The text here is taken out of order. This section of Kimura's book contains individual quotes by Sagawa Sensei that are in no particular order. In the text, the original statement "When you come to understand Aiki…" appears before "By taking the stance…" It was switched in this text only for better flow.

53 Ibid., 51

54 Ibid., 59

55 Ibid., 85

56 Ibid., 151

57 Smith, *Chinese Boxing*

58 Amdur, *Hidden in Plain Sight*

59 Ibid.

60 Stevens, *The Sword of No Sword*, 53

61 All information about Tohei Koichi from this section of the text is from the book *Aikido Pioneers: Pre-War Era*, which contains interviews that Stan Pranin conducted.

62 Misogi is a term used to refer to Japanese esoteric training. Some believe it only encompasses ritual purification using cold water: either meditating underneath freezing waterfalls, or using buckets of cold water for daily ablutions. However, this term is most properly applied to all types of esoteric training.

63 Pranin, *Aikido Pioneers*, 274

64 Ibid.

65 Ibid., 278

66 Ibid.,278.

67 Tohei, *Ki in Daily Life*

68 Ibid.

69 Ibid., 45

70 Ibid., 58

71 This quote was taken from a great compilation at http://www.Aikido-bukitjalil.com/recommended-readings/memoirs-of-o-sensei

72 Friday, *Legacies of the Sword*, 149

73 Yamamoto, *Hagakure*, 1979

GLOSSARY

Acalanatha: a Hindu Deity that later became a Buddhist Guardian King

Aiki: literal translation is "joining energy," but it refers to a coordination of yin and yang

Aikidoka: an Aikido practitioner

Aikijutsu: the art of Aiki. Emphasis is on the use of Aiki, the joining of yin and yang on a contact point, rather than emphasizing jujutsu techniques.

Atavaka: a Hindu Deity that later became a Buddhist Guardian King

Ate: strikes

Atemi: striking (body)

Bokuto: wooden sword

Budo: Literally "martial way," but the character for Bu includes a sword clashing with a spear; the character for the verb "to stop" is underneath, so there is an inherent meaning of "stopping violence."

Chikake: pressure point located at the throat

Chokusen irimi-nage: direct entry throw

Chudan: middle level

Daigensui Myoo: the Japanese name for Atavaka

Dai-itoko Myoo: the Japanese name for Yamantaka

Denkosuei: a pressure point between the second and third ribs

Dojo-yaburi: dojo breaking. This term was used when a challenger showed up at a dojo and defeated the art's practitioners.

Dokko: the pressure point behind the ear in which the jawbone attaches to the skull

Dokkusumi: a pressure point located just under the mastoid process

Emonodori: techniques against a variety of weapons

Fudo Myoo: the Japanese name for Acalanatha

Funa-kogi undo: boat-rowing exercise

Fure-Aiki: literally "touch Aiki," it means "Aiki on contact"

Geta: Japanese-style wooden shoes

Getsuei: pressure point at the edge of the rib cage

Gokyo: technique number five

Gosanze Myoo: the Japanese name for Trailokyavijaya

Happo: eight directions

Happo-giri: eight-direction cuts

Hasso: a position in which the sword or jo is vertical and beside the head. It is also called in no kamae

Hiden mokuroku: A basic series of techniques in Daito-ryu Aikijujutsu

Hiden ogi: A series of techniques in Daito-ryu Aikijujutsu

Hiji-dori: elbow grab

Hiogi: a series of techniques in Daito-ryu Aikijujutsu

Hombucho: the leader of an art's main dojo or headquarters

Horyu: pressure point at the side of the wrist

Ikkajo: the first series in the Daito-ryu Aikijujutsu curriculum of basic techniques

Ikkyo: technique number one

In no kamae: a position in which the sword or jo is vertical and beside the head. It is also called hasso.

Ippondori: Daito-ryu Aikijujutsu's first technique

Irimi: entering (body)

Irimi-nage: entering (body) throw

Isshin: one heart or one mind

Itto: one sword

Jodan: upper level

Jodori: techniques used against attackers who are wielding staffs

Ju yoku go o seisu: a Japanese expression, which means "softness controls hardness"

Kaeshi-waza: counter techniques

Kaiden: A series of techniques in Daito-ryu Aikijujutsu

Kaishaku soden: A series of techniques in Daito-ryu Aikijujutsu

Kaiten-nage: Kaiten is the Japanese word for revolution or rotation, so kaiten-nage is best translated as "rotary throw."

Kamae: stance

Kansetsu: a pressure point found on the thigh

Kasadori: techniques using an umbrella

Kasumi: pressure point located at the temple

Kata: shoulder or form. Although the word refers to both "shoulder" and "form," different Sino-Japanese characters are used for each distinct meaning.

Kata-dori: shoulder grab

Katate-dori: wrist grab. Typically this refers to opposite an opposite side grab. If the defender extends his right hand, for example, the attacker grabs the wrist with his left hand.

Katate-kosa dori: a single-handed, cross-hand wrist grab

Keiko: training

Keikogi: training uniform

Kesa: a surplice or Japanese robe

Kesagiri: a cut at an oblique angle, which would follow the line of a kesa robe

Kiri: cut

Kissaki: sword tip

Kokoro gamae: kokoro means heart or mind and kamae, pronounced as gamae when used in combination with another word, means stance and (in a sense) attitude. These two terms, when together, indicate a mind-body connection and a mindful posture.

Kongoyasha Myoo: the Japanese name for Vajrayaksha

Koryu: old-style Japanese martial arts, which were used on battlefields

Koshi-nage: hip throws

Kote-gaeshi: wrist-twisting or turning technique in Aikido

Kyoju dairi: representative instructor. This is a high-level title bestowed by some traditional Japanese martial arts.

Kyusho: pressure points

Makura no osae: pillow pin

Matsu: pine

Mawasu: a Japanese verb meaning "to turn, rotate, screw, or wind"

Menkyo kaiden: certificate of complete transmission. It signifies that the beholder has learned all techniques and principles in an art.

Morote-dori: a two-handed grab in which the attacker grabs one of nage's wrists with both hands

Mune: chest

Myo: pressure points located aside the nipples

Nage: throw or thrower. Referring to people, these are the practitioners who perform the techniques

Nakayubi ipponken: a strike in which the middle knuckle is raised

Newaza: ground pinning techniques

Nihon nukite: a strike used to target pressure points in which the index finger is over the middle finger, which provides additional support

Nikkajo: the second series in the Daito-ryu Aikijujutsu curriculum of basic techniques

Nikkyo: technique number two

Omote: the seen, what is on the surface, the front

Rokkyo: technique number six

Ryote-dori: two-handed grab. This term is used when the attacker grabs both of the defender's wrists.

Ryuha-bugei: traditional Japanese martial arts

Sankajo: the third series in the Daito-ryu Aikijujutsu curriculum of basic techniques

Sankyo: technique number three

Sen: initiative

Shiho: four directions

Shiho-giri: literally "four-direction cuts"

Shiho-nage: four-directional throw

Shisha: scout

Shitsu: pressure point on the elbow joint

Shodan: beginner's level

Shomenuchi: an attack that issues from straight above

Shoshin: beginner's mind

Shuto: hand-blade. It is also called tegatana.

Sode-dori: sleeve grab

Suigetsu: solar plexus

Suwari-waza: seated techniques

Tachi: sword

Tachidori: techniques against a sword-wielding attackers

Tai sabaki: bodily movements

Taijiquan: a Chinese martial art

Tailu: the Chinese term for "form"

Tai-no-henka: body turning exercise

Take: bamboo

Tasudori: techniques used against group attacks

Tegatana: hand-blade. It is also called shuto.

Tenchi-nage: literally "heaven and earth throw"

Tendo: a pressure point on the top of the head

Trailokyavijaya: a Hindu Deity that later became a Buddhist Guardian King

Tsuki: thrust

Tsurigane: pressure point at the scrotum

Uke: receiver. Typically the one a technique is done to.

Uki-otoshi: floating drop. It is a technique used in Judo.

Ume: plum

Ura: the hidden or the underside

Vajrayaksha: a Hindu Deity that later became a Buddhist Guardian King

Waka: a type of poem found in Japanese classical literature. Sometimes they contain profound teachings.

Yamantaka: a Hindu Deity that later became a Buddhist Guardian King

Yokomenuchi: an attack to the side of the head or neck

Yonkajo: the fourth series in the Daito-ryu Aikijujutsu curriculum of basic techniques

Yonkyo: technique number four

Zaho: seated techniques

BIBLIOGRAPHY

Amdur, E. *Hidden in Plain Sight: Tracing the Roots of Morihei Ueshiba's Power.* Shoreline, WA: Edgework, 2009.

Friday, K. "Off the Warpath: Military Science and Budo in the Evolution of Ryuha Bugei." in *Budo Perspectives*, edited by Alexander Bennett, 249-265. Aukland, New Zealand: Kendo World Publications Ltd., 2005.

Kano, J. *Mind over Muscle: Writings from the Founder of Judo.* Tokyo: Kodansha, 2005.

Kimura, T. *Transparent Power: A Secret Teaching Revealed.* San Fransisco, CA: MAAT Press, 2009.

Li, C., Trans. *A Leap of the Spirit: Moritaka (Morihei) Ueshiba in 1932.* Accessed at http://www.Aikidosangenkai.org/blog/leap-spirit-moritaka-morihei-ueshiba/

Olsen, S. A. *Tai Ji Jin: Discourses on Intrinsic Energies for Mastery of Self-Defense Skills.* Phoenix, Arizona: Valley Spirit Arts, 2013.

Oya, M. "Central Issues in the Instruction of Kendo: With Focus on the Interconnectedness of Waza and Mind." In *Budo Perspectives*, edited by Alexander Bennett, 203-220. Aukland, New Zealand: Kendo World Publications Ltd., 2005.

Pranin, S., Ed. *Aikido Pioneers: Prewar Era.* Kanagawa, Japan: Aiki News, 2010.

Pranin, S. *Ongaeshi: Repaying a Kindness*, 1996, Accessed at https://www.Aikidojournal.com/article?articleID=35.

Shioda, G. *Aikido: My Spiritual Journey.* New York: Kodansha, 2013.

Smith, R. *Chinese Boxing: Masters and Methods*. Berkeley, CA: North Atlantic Books, 1990.

Stevens, J. *The Sword of No-Sword: Life of the Master Warrior Tesshu*. Boston: Shambhala, 1989.

Tohei, K. *Ki in Daily Life*. Tokyo, Japan: Ki no Kenkyukai H.Q., 1978.

Tomiki, K. *Judo, Appendix: Aikido*. (Tourist Library Vol. 22). Tokyo: Japan Travel Bureau, 1959.

Ueshiba, K. *A Life in Aikido: The Biography of Founder Morihei Ueshiba*. (K. Izawa & M. Fuller, Trans.). Tokyo: Kodansha, 2008.

Ueshiba, M. *The Art of Peace*. (J. Stevens, Trans.). Tokyo, Kodansha, 1992.

Ueshiba, M. *Budo: Teachings of the Founder of Aikido*. (J. Stevens, Trans.). Tokyo: Kodansha, 1996.

Wilson, W. S. *The Lone Samurai: The Life of Miyamoto Musashi*. New York: Kodansha, 2004.

Yamamoto, T. *Hagakure: The Book of the Samurai*. Tokyo, Japan: Kodansha, 1979.

www.ingramcontent.com/pod-product-compliance
Lightning Source LLC
Chambersburg PA
CBHW070105120526
44588CB00032B/1076